Solving
the Mysteries
of Breed Type

Richard Beauchamp

Copyright © 2002 by Doral Publishing

All rights reserved. No part of this publication may be reproduced or transmitted in any form or by any means, electronically or mechanically, including photocopying, recording, or by any information storage or retrieval system, without the prior written permission of the publisher.

Published by Doral Publishing, Phoenix, Arizona
Printed in the United States of America.

Edited by Jennifer Bach
Interior Design by The Printed Page
Cover Design by 1106 Design
Cover Photo by Badslage
Cover Dog: Ch. Luzana's Look N' Tri-if-fic
             Owner Janet Langley, Fred Langley, and Carolee Douglas
             Handler Elizabeth Mulvey

Library of Congress Card Number: 2002103420
ISBN: 0-944875-89-0

Publisher's Cataloging-in-Publication
(Provided by Quality Books, Inc.)

Beauchamp, Richard G.
   Solving the mysteries of breed type / by Richard Beauchamp ; Jennifer Bach, editor. -- 1st ed.
   p. cm.
   Includes bibliographical references and index.
   LCCN 2002103420
   ISBN 0-944875-89-0

   1. Dog breeds.   I. Bach, Jennifer. II. Title.

SF426.B43 2002   636.7'1
                          QBI02-200582

Dedication

This book is dedicated to my two greatest mentors, Beatrice Godsol and Derek Rayne—without a doubt two of the most knowledgeable, and at the same time most humble, individuals I have ever had the good fortune of knowing.

Mrs. Beatrice Godsol
William Gilbert photo

Mr. Derek Glennon Rayne
(Courtesy of Derek Rayne, Ltd.

Acknowledgments

The content of this book owes a great deal to Allan Reznik, former editor of the monthly magazine *Dogs In Canada*. It was Allan who found merit in my approach to developing a better understanding of breed type and encouraged me to first present my material as a series of articles in *Dogs In Canada*.

What originally appeared there is supplemented in part by additional material from many of the articles I've written for two other excellent publications: *Dogs In Review*, owned and edited by Bo Bengston and Paul Lipiane, and the United Kennel Club's official publication, *Bloodlines*, edited by Vicki Rand. Both publications have been keenly supportive of my attempts to pass along the storehouse of knowledge I have been fortunate enough to accumulate through my many years involved with purebred dogs.

It would have been impossible to convey my message without the use of the many excellent photographs contained herein. A special note of appreciation is due each and every one of the photographers whose work is included. Our dog show photographers and the photographers who specialize in portraiture record history as it is being made.

And I would be completely remiss if I did not acknowledge the unceasing support and encouragement I have received from that very special person who will remain known simply as "she who knows all"—*priceless!*

Richard Beauchamp

Contents

Looking Forward, Looking Back ix
    The journey xvi
    Globetrotting xvi
Chapter 1. Essentials 3
Accuracy 7
    The preference problem 7
    Inaccurate interpretation 9
    Accuracy and education 9
    Does the ringside count? 10
    Efficient use of time 13
    Parts instead of the whole 14
Logical and just conclusions 15
    Must we all agree? 18
Honesty and courage of convictions 19
    Character and ability 20
    Prejudicial conduct 21
    Roadblocks 21
    Advertising and its effects 22
Sound reasons 23
    How good reasons assist the judge 24
    How good reasons assist the breeder/exhibitor 26
    A true tale 27
    Postscript 28
Chapter 2. Pictures on a Wall 29
    The "Breed Progress Triad" 30
    Selecting the proper tools 31
    Seeing is believing 32
    Developing the picture 34
    A prehistoric art 37
    First the whole 38
    Outcome 39
    Magic formulas 40

Chapter 3. Eliminating the Confusion.............. 43
    A dangerous trend........................ 49
Chapter 4. Defining the Term 55
    The horse before the cart 56
    Statistics—**love 'em or leave 'em** 67
    Who's to blame?........................ 68
    Where type prevails...................... 69
Assignment 72
Chapter 5. The Common Denominators 75
    Origin of beauty points.................... 77
    How much is "too much?".................. 79
    Finding common ground................... 81
    Having an "eye"........................ 82
The five elements of breed type................... 85
    Breed character 85
    Head 86
    Silhouette 86
    Movement 87
    Coat 87
    An overview of the elements................ 88
Chapter 6. Breed Character..................... 89
    Breed character 93
Assignment 108
Chapter 7. Silhouette 109
    Tightening the strings 111
    Breed development 113
    Staying on course....................... 115
    "Horses for courses"..................... 116
    Artist at work.......................... 118
    First impressions....................... 122
    What the silhouette tells us 124
    A case in point 128
    What creates the correct silhouette?.......... 128
    The Davey "five equal parts" Bulldog silhouette.... 130
    Ambiguous terms 131
    Anatomy involved...................... 133
    Common expressions 133
    Determining correct proportions............ 134
    Short necks and long backs 134

    Critical terminology 134
    Disguises 138
    In summary 140
Assignment 140
Chapter 8. Head **141**
    The biggest lie 143
    How important is a breed's head? 145
    Where to begin 146
    Expression 147
    The next step 149
    Head types and typifying expressions 150
    Emphasis 155
    Seeing is believing 155
    Details inside the overall shape. 157
    Flaws and faults are relative 158
    The encompassing shape 159
    The parts 161
    Ear placement and carriage 161
Assignment 164
Chapter 9. Movement **165**
    The three cardinal sins of movement 168
    International concern 174
    To the fastest go the spoils. 176
    Change for change's sake 178
    Then and now 179
Assignment 181
Chapter 10. Coat **183**
    Serviceability, texture and quality 184
    Pattern and distribution 187
    Color. 188
    Markings 188
    Trim 189
    Amount 191
    What does "well-coated" mean? 192
Assignment 198
Chapter 11. The Breed-type Workbook **201**
    The generic landslide 203
    Type, type—who has the type? 205
    Too much 206
    Developing a breed-type workbook 206

Section 1—breed character 207
Section 2—silhouette. 208
Section 3—head 209
Section 4—movement 209
Section 5—coat 209
Chapter 12. The Graphing Technique **211**
Head 216
Movement. 221
Coat 225
In summary 225
Bibliography
Books 227
Magazines. 228
Videos 229
Web Sites 229
National Registry Sources 229
Index **231**

Looking Forward, Looking Back

> *"There is always one moment in childhood when the door opens and lets the future in."*
> Graham Greene
> *The Power and the Glory*

*S*trange, isn't it, the way life unfolds? You'd never expect some minor childhood illness to become a turning point in your life. But as time certainly did prove, this was the case in mine.

I was introduced to the dog game in the most coincidental way. At about nine years old I came down with one of those childhood diseases that run rampant through boarding schools. To tell the truth, I don't recall exactly which of the non-catastrophic afflictions it was. Let's just say it was definitely one of those catchy things that if one student got, they *all* got.

While my classmates were being banished to the infirmary on a daily basis, I somehow managed to hold off on succumbing until I got home for the Christmas holiday. This, of course, totally destroyed my chances of doing any of the things I had planned for months. Instead, I was forced to idle away my vacation days in bed.

It was the early '40s and time of World War II. My stepfather was an officer in the U.S. Navy, serving with the Pacific Fleet. At that moment he was on his way back to our home in Detroit, Michigan, on leave. He was aware of my illness and probably had been advised on the phone by my mother that I was at that stage of recovery where my boredom and restlessness were making life unbearable for her and everyone else within shouting distance. It was long before the advent of television, and in those days parents couldn't keep their children occupied by gluing them to what would become known as "the tube."

"Think of something for him to do," I can imagine her saying, "before he drives us all crazy!" My father's remedy for boredom was a book: Albert Payson Terhune's *Lad—A Dog*. It was the story of a Collie: a Collie so brave, so noble, and so endowed with human qualities, the only thing he didn't do was speak (although I felt he could have, had he been so inclined!). Terhune, in addition to being a breeder and exhibitor of Collies, was a longtime newspaper man and a gifted teller of tales. I was spellbound.

He, his wife, and the dozens of Collies the Terhunes owned lived in what became for me a magical, mystical kingdom called Sunnybank, New Jersey. It was there those super-canines he wrote about performed their feats of derring-do.

An aunt came to visit me just a few days after my father had arrived with book in hand, and she too came bearing gifts for her bedridden nephew. Completely unaware that I was already lost in the world of *Lad*, she had decided to bring a book as well. Her choice was another book by Terhune: *A Dog Named Bruce*.

Fate does have its way!

Lad had hooked me. Bruce reeled me in. I was taken hook, line, and sinker. I would have a Collie, I would breed them, I would show them. They would be my friends, my bosom buddies. They would perform all the same incredible feats for me that the Sunnybank Collies had for Mr. Terhune.

Because of the Sunnybank Collie books, the door to the wonderful world of dogs was opened for me. I entered with the excitement and wonder that only kids can know and experience.

In all the years that have passed since, I've never found any reading material more apt to develop a respect and love for dogs than the Terhune books. They should be a part of every animal-loving family's library.

I realized back then, however, that my dream wasn't to become reality immediately; war, apartment living, food rationing, living away at school—all of these conditions prevailed and prevented any immediate hope of a kennel full of Collies. Still, none of those obstacles prevented me from fantasizing about the day I would have a dog. No, not a dog—many dogs!

I scrimped, saved, and wheedled money out of every member of the family until I owned every single one of the many books in Terhune's series on the Sunnybank dogs. *Lad, Bruce, Treve, Lochinvar Luck*...the list was all but endless. From there I went on to every dog and horse book I could get my hands on.

During those same years I was fortunate to spend considerable vacation time with an uncle who lived nearby. "Uncle Al," an avid hunter and outdoorsman, raised field dogs—English and Irish Setters and Beagles. He became my hero, my substitute Albert Payson Terhune. I was fascinated by my uncle's tales of hunting expeditions and dog lore. I knew everything he said to be true, "the canine gospel according to Uncle Al."

A few years passed, and dog shows, practically at a standstill during the war years, resumed in full swing after peace was declared. I can remember getting on the Woodward Avenue streetcar and riding to the Michigan State Fair Grounds as though it were yesterday. I was on my way to the Detroit Kennel Club's all-breed show. Little did I know as I paid my admission and walked through the turnstile that I was walking into the rest of my life.

Terhune was right. This was unlike anything I had ever known! Dogs were everywhere, of every make, shape, and kind imaginable. I was bedazzled, awestruck by the beauty of some of the breeds and at the same time amazed that anyone could be attracted to some of the others, which were nothing short of grotesque as far as I was concerned.

I spent hours trudging from one trade stand to another, collecting pound after pound of dog food samples for my dog-to-be. Eventually I gathered up enough courage to start asking questions of the people sitting in front of the dogs chained to their benches.

The people sitting there spoke to each other nonstop, it seemed, and in a language that I understood only snippets of—a language that was English but at the same time not. Their conversation contained so many strange words, I felt very much on the outside looking in.

They were, of course, speaking in terms used by experienced breeders—conversations that the non-initiated might make little sense of but in the end are responsible for shaping the future of many a breed.

In those days—before the general use of magazines to publicize dogs—breeders and exhibitors used stud cards and brochures to describe their individual dogs and their breeding programs. They passed these out as they sat all day in front of their benches at the shows. Those I collected on that first day were treasured keepsakes for many years: Knightscroft Irish Setters and Dachshunds, Tokalan Cockers, Blue Bar English Setters, Frejax Springers, Stonewall Norwegian Elkhounds, Honey Hollow Great Danes. As baseball cards are to kids of today's generation, so were these wonderfully illustrated and descriptive kennel cards and brochures to me.

One woman, who sat in front of what I was sure was the most beautiful Collie I had ever seen, told me she had puppies at home whose father had come to America from Scotland. She handed me a picture of the dog, and I realized that while her benched dog was beautiful, the dog in the picture was even more so. She also told me that she had driven all the way to Pompton Lakes, New Jersey, to breed to the dog in the picture because she said it was, as I recall, "the typiest Collie that's ever been."

I hadn't a clue to what she meant by "typiest" but wasn't about to let on how much of a novice I was. I stored the word and found that it would become the most frequently and most arbitrarily used of any I would hear for as long as I was to remain involved with purebred dogs.

Interesting, isn't it, the things you remember and the things you don't? My parents feared I'd be in college before I memorized my multiplication tables. But dog lingo and pedigrees—I was like a sponge! One or two readings of a four-generation pedigree, and I could rattle off the whole thing without a hitch.

But back to our dog show....

As my knowledge of the dog-show world grew, I learned that the dog pictured was Ch. Braegate Model of Bellhaven, the Collie who was shown forty times and remained undefeated in the breed. Model had won many Working Groups, including Westminster Kennel Club, and even two all-breed Bests in Show in the days when Collies did not do such things.

Looking Forward, Looking Back xiii

This picture was given to me at my first dog show—the Detroit Kennel Club, sometime in the late 1940s. The dog was Ch. Braegate Model of Bellhaven, who remains a Collie icon to this day. Model was imported and owned by Mrs. Florence Bell Ilch of Red Bank, New Jersey. Her Bellhaven-bred dogs served as the foundation for countless producing lines. I was fascinated by something in the picture that at that time I was unable to fully appreciate. That "something" proved to be a sense of stockmanship—an appreciation for a fine animal—that I have come to believe I inherited from the British side of my own pedigree. (Tauskey photo)

Later in the day I noted that something important appeared to be going on in the center of the building. The spectators stood three deep around the ring. I wound my way through the crowd and saw a whole ring of what I recognized as "hunting dogs": Setters, Pointers, and Spaniels. I recognized them because of my uncle.

I found a seat in the gallery and took in the scene: a judge, a big red Irish Setter, and an orange and white English Setter. The English, even to my untrained eye, was stunning—vaguely reminiscent of the dogs my uncle used in the field, but somehow this dog seemed to have so much more of everything. I was fascinated.

When the judge had the English move down the center of the ring, the ringside came to its feet and roared its approval. The glamour and presence of the dog and the electricity of the moment sent chills along my arm!

And it was at that moment that I heard the word "type" used for the second time. The man sitting next to me turned to the lady he was sitting with and said, "I still like the Irish, but my God, the type on the English!"

I wondered how both a Collie and an English Setter could both have this "type" thing. One looked nothing like the other.

The English Setter was no less than the marvelous Ch. Rock Falls Colonel (and, yes, he did win the Sporting Group that night in Detroit). At the time of his retirement at the great Morris & Essex show in May 1957, "the Colonel," as everyone referred to him, had won 160 other Group Firsts as well as 101 all-breed Bests in Show—an unheard-of accomplishment in that day. He had broken, by 1, the Best in Show record that had been set by the mighty Peke winner Ch. Chik T'Sun of Caversham.

The English Setter Ch. Rock Falls Colonel, bred, owned, and handled by William T. Holt of Richmond, Virginia. "The Colonel" was a product of the breed's "Golden Age" that existed throughout the 1940s and 1950s. They were banner decades for the English Setters across the country. This said much for English Setter breeders in that the Sporting Group was at an all-time high in overall quality at that time. The high level of those years had a profound influence on my education in dogs. (Evelyn M. Shafer photo)

I remember being very happy when he broke the record in that I was definitely a Colonel groupie and totally convinced that an English Setter was better than some old Peke anyway!

The Colonel's descendants dominated the breed for generations to come, and his record stands unchallenged in the breed to this day.

Every once in a while I pull out the photograph I have of the Colonel—a treasured gift from the dog's owner, Bill Holt—to see if the dog was as wonderful as I remember. I am never disappointed. Here was a dog that clearly illustrated the old dog term, "a successful sum of all the parts."

The classic elegance of his exquisite head, his overall balance, the angles, the ease at which one portion of his anatomy flowed on to the next and allowed him to float around the ring—all sheer perfection. Add to this a ring presence that commanded every eye, and you have what all who breed or show or judge keep looking for—that once-in-a-lifetime dog that makes all the rest of the effort worth working through. Although I had no idea at the time, I had been introduced to a dog who not only *had*—but *was*—*type*.

The magnificent Pekingese Ch. Chik T'Sun of Caversham was the dog of the hour, the day, the month, the year, if not the entire decade, when I began going to shows. I knew nothing of Pekes, but even back in those early years I couldn't help but be impressed by both the dog and the talent of his handler, Clara Alford. Chik T'Sun had been imported from England by Nigel Aubrey-Jones and R. William Taylor and was later sold to Mr. & Mrs. Charles Venable of Atlanta, Georgia. He was the top-winning show dog of all time until Ch. Rock Falls Colonel topped by one the standing record of one hundred all-breed Bests in Show. (Frasie photo)

The journey

All this took place over fifty years ago. Ironically, I never did get my Collie, although there have been a good number of other breeds in the interim. Perhaps it's just as well—I doubt any Collie, or any breed of dog, for that matter, could live up to the magic of the Sunnybank Collies, and anything less would have been a disappointment. What I did get, though, has lasted a lifetime. My journey through the dog world has taken me through the realms of breeder, exhibitor, judge, and journalist. Along that fascinating way I've had the unique good fortune of being able to sit and talk with the greatest dog men and women of our time—not only here at home but around the world as well.

Globetrotting

I was there in Sydney, Australia, while Harry Spira was working on his critically acclaimed book, *Canine Terminology*. It was to my delight and benefit that Cam Milward, breeder of the world-renowned Grenpark Smooth Fox Terriers, sat me down one fine day and told me where he thought I was on (and off!) in judging his breed at one of Melbourne's important shows.

One of the most memorable afternoons I've ever spent in all these years in dogs was at Rossut, the home of Group Captain "Beefy" Sutton and his famous wife, Catherine. I was in England for Crufts, partially to cheer on a very young man at the time, Simon Briggs, who that year was competing for the World Junior Handler award scheduled to be judged by American Ann Stevenson. (Simon did take top honors that year.)

I had met Simon a year earlier, when I judged the West Australia Junior Showman competition in Perth. He was my overall winner, and he went on to win the Australian finals under Edd and Irene Bivin later that year at the Melbourne Royal show. Simon's knowledge and ability with dogs so impressed me that we established and maintained a friendship that lasted through the years.

The Suttons had invited Simon and me for the day, and we were joined there by our friends Geoff Corish and Michael Coad, who were also the Suttons' highly successful handlers, Geoff having won Best in Show at Crufts on several different occasions with dogs of different breeds.

Australia's Simon Briggs was part of a most memorable day at Captain and Mrs. Sutton's Rossut Farm in England. By far the youngest member of our group that day, Briggs conceded little in the dog knowledge department. A handler par excellence, he would go on to join with Norma Hamilton to campaign the Quailmoor Irish Setters to great records Down Under. He is pictured here with one of the many Quailmoor winners, Ch. Jumpin' Jack Flash. (Cabal photo).

I was a great fan of Mrs. Sutton's from the time she had come to America to judge at Santa Barbara Kennel Club. I watched her do a splendid job in a number of breeds, and she had earned my unending admiration when she placed George and Sally Bell's Saluki, Ch. Bel S'mbran Fantasia, as Best in Show over an incredibly formidable lineup of dogs. Fantasia had been a major winner of the period and one of my personal favorites. Mrs. Sutton's decision could not possibly have pleased me more.

I was fascinated by Mrs. Sutton's knowledge of the countless breeds we discussed and in awe of her ability to capture in just a few words what was in effect the absolute essence of the breeds she talked about. Coad and Corish were equally adept at doing so, and I vowed to shift my priorities from showmanship and charisma to type.

The travesty was that the day's conversation was not recorded! We left no stone and no dog unturned, and I was amazed to see that in spite of country, involvement, age, or breed preferences, we all saw quality in the same way.

*I first met Catherine Sutton when she came to America to judge at the famed Santa Barbara Kennel Club show. Mrs. Sutton finished judging her huge Borzoi assignment late in the day and came to tell me she had just put up to Best of Breed what was, in her opinion, one of the greatest Borzois she had ever seen. The dog was Dyane Roth's Ch. Kishniga's Dalgarth. Mrs. Sutton was scheduled to do Best in Show, and there was no doubt in my mind who would win it. However, that was **before** Jim Clark judged the Hound Group and put one of my own personal favorites, the SalukiCh. Del S'mbran Fantasia, first and the Borzoi second! No chance for the Saluki for Best under those circumstances, one would think. Mrs. Sutton, on the other hand, did not let her disappointment stand in the way of her objectivity and gave the nod to the Saluki. (Missy photo)*

Mrs. Sutton and I plotted that day to bring about the mating of England's Ch. Tiopepi Mad Louie at Pamplona and America's Ch. Devon Puff And Stuff—the world's two leading Bichon winners at the time. Unfortunately, quarantine regulations worked against us, and the breeding never took place. I think to this day it was unfortunate for the breed on both sides of the Atlantic that it did not.

I was spellbound by the experiences and knowledge of Italy's Paolo Dondino while we traveled through Finland on a judging tour. While there, we were given a glimpse of the obviously successful manner in which Finland trains its judges—a sterling example provided by the internationally respected Finnish judging trio Hans Lehtinen, Kari Jarvinen, and Reiner Voorhinen.

Chapter Looking Forward, Looking Back xix

The Bichon Frise had already caught on like wildfire in the United States in the early 1980s. It was my distinct pleasure in 1986 to give Michael Coad's and Geoff Corishes' outstanding Ch. Tiopepi Mad Louie at Pamplona the win at Scottish Kennel Club that would earn him his first Best in Show. The Messrs. Coad and Corish did much to establish the Bichon breed as formidable competition in the United Kingdom. (David Lindsay photo)

Judging at the famed Leeds dog show in England put me on the same panel as Finland's world-famous judging trio: Reiner Voorhinen, Hans Lehtinen, and Kari Jarvinen. I had met them in Helsinki a few years prior and was fascinated by their explanation of the Finnish Kennel Club's judges-training program. The ability of these three alone stands in testimony of the excellence of the system to this day. (Photo by the author)

Canada, South Africa, South America, New Zealand, and Japan—all have contributed heavily to what we have and know here in the United States. Collectively they have provided me with an education far surpassing any I could have hoped for or ever imagined that day I walked through the turnstile at the Detroit Kennel Club.

My first trip to South Africa to judge the Goldfield Kennel Club's all-breed show inspired the local press to do a feature on "Hollywood Dog Judge Comes to Johannesburg." As I stepped off the plane, the first question I got was, "OK, who really shot J. R.?" Evidently my hosts were much bigger fans of TV's Dallas *than I was because my naive response was, "J. R. who?"*

As editor and publisher of *Kennel Review* magazine for over thirty years I was also directly involved in the promotional campaigns of a vast majority of the great winners of that era. I became privy to a great deal of the knowledge and experience that was invested in the winning and producing success of the dogs owned by our clients. Few really appreciate the talent involved in shaping the careers of these dogs that make history.

My status as an all-breed judge in countries governed by the Federacion Cynologique Internationale gave me an incredibly broad picture of the world's dog scene and the breeds in it. It also gave me an opportunity to judge alongside many of the world's great international judges—an experience I consider without equal. This judging experience put me in touch with the variations that time and distance can create within our breeds.

This lifelong and multi-layered experience in the world of dogs taught me one monumentally important lesson—the more fully an individual understands the meaning of the term "breed type," the more effective and successful the person will be in any chosen purebred-related endeavor.

My purpose then in writing this book is twofold: to pass along what I've learned and to provide a key to understanding what excellence in purebred dogs actually means. The only compensation my mentors wanted in return for what they gave was a promise from me to one day do the same for the generations that would follow.

Hopefully this book will also help to clear away the ambiguity that surrounds that important term "breed type." A full understanding of what this really means can't help but provide greater access to understanding what separates quality from mediocrity and elevates an individual dog or breeding program to excellence.

The greater our understanding of the nuances of excellence, the better our ability to fulfill our responsibilities as breeder, judge, or exhibitor. In doing so we help preserve the intent of the founders of our given breeds and assist in the selection of stock that will best accommodate that goal.

Let's begin our journey.

Richard G. (Rick) Beauchamp

Part I

The Enigma of Breed Type

1 Essentials

*O*ne of the most fascinating things about the dog game is that its changes have no end. Without a doubt it is the ideal avocation for those of us inclined to lose interest in the static. Every new avenue of dog knowledge you explore opens the door to new roads you had not thought to investigate.

I can't tell you how often I've thought to myself, "What in the world does anyone see in that breed?" and then wound up totally immersing myself in it. The dog game is one in which anyone involved should be very careful about saying *never*.

In fact, one characteristic I find common among those who succeed in their chosen segment of the dog game is what I call "all-breed mindedness"—an interest to a greater or lesser degree in all breeds of dogs.

Most of us who have been involved with purebred dogs for many years are thoroughly convinced you don't fully understand your own breed until you can begin to compare what you know to other breeds. The ability to do this seems typical of what produces master breeders and individuals who eventually become our best judges. Understanding breeds other than our own allows us to see why certain characteristics exist and to what degree they are called for in our own breed.

It should come as no surprise that this all-breed interest is a characteristic of both our top breeders and our top judges. There is little difference in what they do other than where and when. Judges do their selecting in the ring; breeders, in the whelping box.

The judge usually does selecting on weekends, while the breeder, consciously or unconsciously, is doing judging day in and day out. A good breeder begins judging the minute a litter is born and does not stop the evaluating process until his or her last dog is retired. "Which of this litter of six is the best puppy? Which is second best? Which, if any, have no redeeming virtues?" These are questions every breeder must ask, and they are the same questions that every judge asks of every class he or she passes upon.

This is not to say that the person who comes from the ranks of the professional handler is not called upon to evaluate. Any person with a good hand on a dog has a distinct advantage in the ring and gains respect for having that talent. However, the person who understands and is concerned with type is then more able to separate the wheat from the chaff. This individual is far more apt to have a top-notch string and earn greater respect and success than someone who merely shows what he or she has been handed with no respect to what might be of value to the breed.

The longer people breed and watch puppies grow and mature, the more proficient they will be in evaluating what stands before them. Realistically, however, this is all well and good for a person's first breed, but we certainly can't expect someone to have bred and raised every single breed he or she might want to understand or judge. At that rate, most people would be far along into senility before they came anywhere near being able to judge more than a handful of breeds. How, then, do people go about expanding their knowledge of an entirely new breed without the benefit of a breeding program?

In a word, the key to learning any breed is research. Through the years I have made it a practice to clip and save articles from dog newspapers and magazines that deal with breed type and soundness and movement as they relate to a specific breed. After the articles have been read, and on some occasions certain areas highlighted, I file the articles alphabetically by breed. At first there is a general file for each letter of the alphabet, but as soon as I have acquired sufficient material on a single breed I give that breed its own individual folder. I also include pictures of outstanding dogs in this file.

Breed standards can and do differ from country to country, but nevertheless, all valuable information is kept regardless of the country in which the writer might live. You will find there is always some bit of valuable information that applies in well-written articles by people who really know their breed. Often, articles from the foreign press bring to mind facts that have been obscured in the breed's development (or changed!) as it has moved from country to country.

Chapter 1

There are some breeds that have a great number (some good, some not so good) and others that really some diligent searching to come by. Do spend some time through a book before before you buy it. Just because appear on the printed page, they are not necessarily written by individuals who have the knowledge you are after.

There is also a great deal to be learned from books that are more generally applicable than those written for a specific breed. I do feel that they should come *after* you have a good sense of what your own breed is all about. Although the *principles* that apply to construction and movement remain the same for all breeds, correct *construction* of the individual breeds is what determines how those principles will operate.

No dog library should call itself complete without copies of books such as *The Dog in Action* by McDowell Lyon (Orange Judd Publishing Company, Inc.) and Rachel Page Elliott's *Dogsteps* (Doral Publishing). The Lyon book is out of print, but odd copies may be found at dog show book stalls or occasionally in used bookstores.

Books of this nature are primers on the general principles of correct movement and will prove to be a ready reference for one's entire life in dogs, whether that life is as a breeder or a judge. The two cover their subject matter well, but it is wise to consult with experts in your own breed to see where and how the principles discussed in these or other general books apply.

There are two other books that I can highly recommend. The first is Mary Roslin Williams's book, originally titled *Advanced Labrador Breeding* (H. F. & G. Witherby, Ltd.). The breeding and judging advice included in this gem have proven so valuable to all breeds that its general content has been republished under the title *Reach for the Stars* (Doral Publishing, Inc.).

The other book on my "must" list has nothing at all to do with dogs but a whole lot to do with the process of evaluation. The title is *Dairy Cattle Judging Techniques* by George Trimberger, William M. Etgen, and David M. Galton (Waveland Press). The qualities that a good livestock judge—amateur or professional—must possess are analyzed in this book and prove as applicable to dogs as to livestock of any kind.

Livestock judges are required to give reasons for every animal they judge. In dog parlance we call these reasons "critiques." Many people can tell you they like or dislike a dog, but when it comes to stating specific reasons for this opinion, their response may not be based on sound judgment. Practice at making specific critiques can hone one's ability to eliminate superfluous details and get down to the real essence of a breed. Whether the critiques are ever seen by anyone else is immaterial, but should you have the good fortune of being able to share your analysis with a knowledgeable friend, so much the better.

There is nothing more helpful to the student than having someone with longtime experience and great knowledge offer to take on the role of mentor. Although the mentor cannot learn *for* you, your mentor can show you the correct path to follow, and it is extremely beneficial to have someone to turn to when the inevitable questions arise.

No one, no matter how brilliant, starts with as much knowledge of a breed as he or she will have gained after years of experience with that breed. The reason, quite simply, is that evaluating dogs is an art, and like any artistic endeavor, it takes time.

If you have a real desire to learn to understand and become proficient in evaluating dogs, there is no doubt you can accomplish that goal. You have to understand that some people can do so more quickly than others, and some will develop the ability to a greater degree than others. That's life, as the old saying goes, and is the result of our being human beings and not machines.

The ultimate goal is to be able to recognize breed type in each new breed you approach. There are certain essentials that support a person's ability to do so. If you understand them and make them a part of your approach to purebred dogs, you can't help but provide the foundation necessary for proficiency.

The essentials of sound evaluation are:

- Accuracy
- Logical and just conclusions
- Honesty and courage of convictions
- Sound reasoning

We have seminars and workshops that tell us what is right and wrong in our breeds every month of the year and from one coast to the other. However, there aren't any schools that dog fanciers can attend to acquire the critical knowledge that will allow them to recognize and properly apply these rights and wrongs. This is something that can't be learned in a matter of hours or even days or weeks, for that matter.

The ability to apply the essentials of sound evaluation can take many years of study and comparison and often involves major adjustments as time passes. Some essentials are the result of an individual's personal standards and just as often reflect a person's level of integrity.

They are very real, however, and if it is possible for an individual to fully understand each and every one of these essentials before taking on the major responsibility of breeding or judging, I feel certain that individual will be miles ahead in his or her pursuit of knowledge. We'll take a look at these essentials one at a time so that they are clearly understood by anyone who might have aspirations to evaluate their own breed more effectively or to learn a new breed.

Accuracy

The preference problem

It is extremely important in evaluating dogs that the person doing so is making accurate decisions. This sounds like simply part and parcel of the evaluating experience; one would think that everyone who knows a given breed will at least attempt to be accurate to the best of their ability. Unfortunately, this can prove easier said than done.

One of the biggest stumbling blocks to accuracy is allowing *what we like,* as individuals, to stand in the way of something else that is equally correct and fully acceptable in a breed. For instance, in the case of a standard that allows a wide range of size, as many of our standards do, some individuals will arbitrarily decide they *like* only the very smallest or the very largest. The liking part is fine, but it should never stand in the way of appreciating a fine dog that may not fit our personal size *preference.* So long as the dog in question falls within the parameters set down by the standard, all sizes must be given equal consideration and decisions made only on overall quality.

Accuracy in evaluating her breed was one of Norma Hamilton's outstanding qualities when she was actively breeding and showing the Quailmoor Irish Setters. She was keenly observant of the differences that existed in dogs of her breed bred in the United States and those bred in Great Britain. Rather than operating from "preference," Norma used a discriminating eye to determine where the dogs of each country excelled and sought to combine the best of each in her own line. Her efforts found approval from judges and breeders from the four corners of the world. She is pictured here with just one example of this breeding accuracy—the outstanding winner and producer Ch. Quailmoor Jumpin' Jack Flash. (Cabal photo)

In cases like the size issue, a judge is only afforded the luxury of implementing personal preference when it comes to a matter of two dogs of equal quality (which most of us who judge know is a rare instance indeed) and there is no other reason for deciding between one and the other.

The breeder is equally at liberty to have a size preference and set up a breeding program to accommodate this end as long as it falls within the parameters of the breed standard. The problem that all too frequently arises is that preferences of this nature develop into obsessions. The breeders are unable to appreciate good dogs—theirs or others'—that do not fall within their range of preferences.

Operating within this form of restricted vision serves as a real handicap to the breeder's own breeding program. Further, and often unfortunately, many breeders of this persuasion are apt to try and influence others to abide by their own self-imposed restrictions. This can have detrimental effects upon other breeding programs and the breed itself.

Inaccurate interpretation

If decisions are based entirely on personal preferences, a person risks inaccurately interpreting the standard of the breed. Another example of this nature might be seen in allowable colors. A standard may read, "Any color—solid, marked, or splashed—in any configuration is acceptable." To give preference to or reject parti-color or solid or brindle dogs simply because of their color is, again, an inaccurate interpretation of the standard.

Later, when the breeder becomes a judge, it can be extremely difficult for the individual to get by biases and prejudices when passing judgment in the ring. In truth, it would be surprising if a breeder-judge did not walk into the ring with some biases. After all, a breeder knows only too well how many years it took to perfect or get rid of some characteristic in his or her own line. However, it is important to be sure *the standard* places no more or no less emphasis on that characteristic than on any other.

Accuracy and education

I wonder how many realize the educational benefit good ring procedure can have for the exhibitor and ringside observer who are in a good many cases our breeders? Every dog entered should be examined in the same way and in a manner that is appropriate for that particular breed. This is not only for the sake of fairness but to make sure something is not overlooked in the process.

Although some judges examine each dog in the class with great care, they wait far too long to begin making cuts that will assist them in arriving at which dogs, in the end, will constitute their final placements. In a very large class this can end in total confusion for the judge, and someone interested in the judge's opinion would have no idea how final conclusions were reached. Attending to a large entry in a systematic fashion not only eliminates such confusion, it helps those interested in the judge's opinion see what the statement being made actually is.

As each dog is given its thorough examination and has been moved individually, the judge begins to see that each successive dog is either better than or of lesser quality than the one that came before it. Many judges believe it helps considerably to start creating some order of preference as they go, rather than waiting until after all the dogs have been examined.

In a large class, it is very easy to forget a fault on one of the early dogs. On the other hand, the dog that does not appeal at all on the setup may be suffering from bad handling rather than a lack of quality.

Eliminating the dogs not in consideration after the initial examination begins to sketch out the judge's picture of the ideal. It's a "good ones up front, poor ones at the end" approach. The first cut a more general picture, and as each dog moves forward in consideration, a more detailed portrait emerges of what the judges consider quality.

Systematic "cuts" on the part of the judge (reducing and eliminating the number of competing dogs) assists the judge in avoiding confusion and conveys to ringside observers where his or her preferences lie. It seems only reasonable to assume that after giving initial examination to each dog in a class of twenty, a judge would not still be considering all twenty for the four final placements. Systematic elimination over time also allows the breeder to be more accurate in selecting the best puppies in a litter. (Author photo)

Does the ringside count?

Some judges do not feel they owe spectators anything at all. In many instances they give no clue where they are heading until there is a sudden, "One—two—three—four" and the ribbons are handed out. Neither spectator nor exhibitor is given any idea how, out of a large class, the judge arrived at the four finalists. I call this the "popcorn approach"—the judge stares and stares until four placements suddenly come bursting out. The correctness of the judge's choices is certainly not being questioned here, only the procedure used to arrive at them.

I, like a good number of other judges, feel what we do can be an educational experience for all present both in and out of the ring. Following initial examination, judges who see what they do as an educational process may reduce a class of twenty to, say, a much handier and more observable ten. (It does not seem reasonable that after the initial examination the judge would still be considering all twenty.) This gives the observer the opportunity to see which ten of the twenty the judge feels come closer to his or her interpretation of the standard.

As additional observation of the ten remaining dogs is then made, moving forward those that stand foremost in consideration draws an even clearer picture of what the judge is after. Final arrangement of the top four in descending order before the last pass around the ring gives observers an opportunity to see exactly what the judge has interpreted as closest to the standard. It should be obvious this system would paint a much more vivid and less mistake-prone picture of the judges' interpretation of the standard than the popcorn method.

Although some judges feel they owe spectators nothing other than what is revealed in their final placements, other judges do their best to educate in the manner in which they conduct their ring and examine their dogs. Here, multiple group judge Frank Sabella examines the famed Smooth Fox Terrier sire and show dog Ch. Ttarb The Brat. Although a dog of this breed hides little from the observer, Sabella's hands make it perfectly clear what he is checking for, and without unnecessary flourish or wasted motion he conveys that message to interested observers. (Photos by the author)

Efficient use of time

It is a mistake to think that the longer one spends on making a decision, the more accurate that decision will be. I personally believe the contrary to be true. Prolonging decisions unnecessarily can lead to confusion, and when this occurs in the ring, it appears the person attempting to make the decisions is indecisive.

Even when culling litters I have found that the initial assessment proves valuable—the puppy that stands out above the rest is most apt to have more of the best. Constant overanalyzing of what is or what might be a failure leads to more erratic decision making than is necessary.

While I was still actively conducting a breeding program, I occasionally sold a particularly good female back with the proviso that I would get my choice of puppy back when she was bred. I seldom found myself in conflict concerning what the owner of the litter had decided to keep. The owner's choice was all too often based on overanalyzing the litter so that he or she became bogged down in details rather than simply picking what was obviously the standout puppy.

Straight shoulders or a low tail set are just that and will not change simply because you have checked them time and time again. It is wise to remember that a dog is what it is. No amount of staring is going to change anything. It will be the same dog or puppy the first time you look at it or go over it as it will be twenty minutes later. Actually, it may wind up being less through no fault of its own but because it has become exhausted waiting for you to make up your mind!

Comparing one dog's movement to another's makes sense. Comparing one dog's movement to that of every other dog in the class or litter makes no sense at all. A dog moves as it moves, period, and for a judge to compare the dog he or she has in mind for first place with a dog not being considered at all proves nothing and does nothing but waste time.

I have never been an advocate of moving more than one dog a time when it comes to comparison. The eye can only watch one dog at a time, so why bother having two move at once? It only serves to interfere with both dogs' concentration and the way they will perform.

Parts instead of the whole

Too much time observing a class can cause other problems as well. I have seen judges' eyes drawn to the best dog in the class as it entered the ring, but a belabored decision-making process made them see parts instead of the whole; they lost what in fact should have been an easy winner.

It will undoubtedly take you longer to judge a breed the first time than it will many assignments later. This is understandable. New judges are normally unsure of themselves and have not learned to rely upon an efficient system of handling the ring, so part of their concentration is on procedure rather than on decision making. Implementing the same system over and over will considerably shorten time spent.

The new judge has not had time to decide or to research where concessions can and cannot be made. This prolongs decision making as well. But in the case of judging dogs, practice, in fact, does make perfect. (Well, if not "perfect," at least "improved.")

Logical and just conclusions

Before going on, I feel it is important to remind the reader that the essentials to good judgment are not confined solely to the person who makes decisions on a formal basis in a show ring. Evaluating dogs is evaluating dogs, whether you are standing inside the ring or at home looking at that new litter in the whelping box.

The breeder is called upon to make the same judgments every step of the way on the road to success. First, he or she must obtain a foundation bitch. Then the breeder must select the proper sire for the bitch when it is time to breed her. When the litter arrives, the breeder must employ these essentials to determine which, in fact, are the best puppies in the litter and separate them from those that are purely companion stock. Nor does it end there. When the breeder-cum-exhibitor walks into the ring, he or she should be able to assess the competition clearly and objectively so as to avoid the embarrassment of crying "foul" when the decision goes to another dog. So, you see, these essentials are no less important for the responsible breeder than they are for the appointed judge of the day.

But let us now move on to developing the ability to arrive at logical and just conclusions. A judge may have a crystal-clear picture of what ideal type is in a given breed. This person may also be extremely accurate in assessing the dogs presented, but none of that will lead to placing the dogs in proper order if the judge cannot do so with logic and be truly justified in arriving at those decisions.

This requires an ability to weigh and balance the qualities and shortcomings of one dog against those of its competitors.

This has been best explained by Mary Roslin Williams in *Reach for the Stars*.

Williams approaches the problem of being logical and arriving at just conclusions by first warning the evaluator to avoid fault judging at all costs. It is her opinion that a person who fault judges in or out of the ring is "looked upon with contempt," both by those who are truly experienced in the realm of judging and by those who are simply knowledgeable dog persons.

This does not mean to dispense with faults—on the contrary—but to begin eliminating dogs from consideration by faults could easily have you dismiss the best dog in the first cut. One of my own mentors warned me early on, "Any damn fool can spot a fault. It takes breed knowledge to appreciate the qualities of a dog." The late Mrs. Beatrice Godsol, a legend among great judges, expressed the same thought in perhaps a more ladylike fashion by saying, "All dogs have faults; the great ones just carry them well."

But I have digressed. Let's get back to Williams and her book. Williams goes on to suggest that we should learn to differentiate between "faults"and "failings." She describes faults as "constructional" and failings as "cosmetic." In other words, faults are those things that stand in the way of a dog being what the breed was intended to be.

For example, a thirty-pound Pomeranian could simply not be what the breed was intended to be—a Toy. Nor could a long-headed, pencil-necked dog parade as a Bulldog. The heritage of the Bulldog demands exceptional jaw strength and a powerful neck. A Sporting Dog or Hound with weak, splayed feet and weak pasterns could never stand up to its role as a field dog, and, obviously, this is a fault.

On the other hand, Williams would regard things such as too large or small an ear, too light or dark an eye, or even something like lack of brilliant showmanship as "failings." These are things that a very good dog could fall short in, and still it would have to be considered among the top dogs in its class. Again, there are some failings we do not like or do not want in our line that may be present in dogs we look at, but we must be careful to be logical in the manner in which we weigh the particular flaw or flaws against the overall quality of the dog.

A classic example of such objectivity can be found in a critique written by Charles Mason, one of the past's most knowledgeable dog men. In 1888 he wrote a book titled *Our Prize Dogs*. He included critiques of every dog to which he had awarded a prize in his many assignments throughout the East.

Among those critiques was one written after he had passed upon a huge entry of Smooth Fox Terriers at an important show. "Lucifer," Mason's Best of Breed dog at that event, was a leading winner of the day and was owned by the influential August Belmont. The critique Mason wrote read, in part, as follows:

> "Skull of excellent formation...cheeks showing slight fullness. Muzzle clearly cut, neat, and strong in lower jaw, but showing slight weakness an inch or so from the eyes. Ears of exquisite formation, perfect in carriage and position, and of sterling quality. Teeth sound and level.
>
> "We now come to the dog's one and only defect—his eyes. In size, position and formation they are as nearly perfect as we expect to ever find, but in color they are without exception the worst that we have ever seen in a noted first prize winner. In nine cases out of ten, eyes like Lucifer's would utterly destroy the character of the dog's face; and it is a strong point in his favor that notwithstanding his great drawback he still shows intense and unmistakable character. Neck formed on beautiful lines. Shoulder long, clean, sloping and well laid back.... An active, strong, well-built, racy looking terrier showing much character and lovely quality. He is undoubtedly the best Fox Terrier dog that has been exhibited in America."

What a gift to be able to maintain one's objectivity in light of a fault that is so glaring—"the worst that we have ever seen." However, when Mason balanced that blatant fault against the dog's many virtues, he could not deny the win! It is important that both breeders and judges ask themselves whether they all could be as objective.

In many of our very old standards, there were points awarded to the various characteristics of given breeds—so many points for head, so many for coat, etc. This was very effective in educating the person who was attempting to learn the breed to emphasize the more important aspects of a breed. However, the down side of the point scores was that too many students would evaluate the dog entirely on the basis of those high-point characteristics at the expense of all others.

Certainly a Collie's head is an extremely important part of the breed's essence, but judging the entire dog on head quality alone and ignoring the fact that this is a Herding Dog would present a grave injustice to the breed.

Then, too, some of the old standards scored certain characteristics with a high number that without a doubt were important to the breed, but judges would drop dogs from consideration and deduct all points because the dog failed in some aspects of that quality. Would it be fair for a Toy breed with a level bite (whose standard called for a scissors bite) to have all the points for bite taken away? After all, in dog parlance, does not the term "bite" include teeth of a specific kind in a given order and of a specified number

These are the situations that the responsible breeder and judge must consider and for which they must arrive at logical and just conclusions. The person who is able to do this is far more apt to gain respect and success not only as a breeder but also as a judge.

A respected breeder would not breed or show a dog with a major fault, nor would a judge intentionally give a dog with a major fault a high award. Both would prefer not to have a dog with shortcomings but would understand that it would not make good sense to deny the dog because it failed in some lesser respect.

It may be difficult for some to differentiate between these first two essentials that we have dealt with—accurate assessment and using logic in arriving at conclusions—but that is understandable. The two are interrelated, and in fact one is extremely difficult to implement without use of the other.

Must we all agree?

If every person were to develop the ability to efficiently employ these first two essentials of evaluating, would they all make exactly the same decisions? The answer is, quite clearly, no! This will never be the case, quite simply because we are dealing with human beings. No two humans will ever perceive all things in life in exactly the same manner.

Granted, when it comes to what we have referred to as faults in our dogs, it is of great importance that we all recognize them as just that. In the case of our field dogs, anyone who would not severely penalize bad feet and legs simply does not understand what is essential to a dog that works the day long over rough terrain.

No, what I am talking about here is the way we might perceive a dog's shortcomings. Our backgrounds, our experience, and the degree to which we employ our appreciation for the aesthetic qualities of a breed will all figure into our evaluation of a particular failing. Being a bit off color may not eliminate the dog from the consideration of Judge A, but if he has a dog in the ring that is as good as the off-color entry and is also of absolutely correct color, one need not be a rocket scientist to figure out which dog will win. This color thing may not bother Judge B nearly as much, so she might just as easily choose either dog.

And thus we have different opinions and constantly have different dog shows. If all judges agreed to the letter, there would be no need for any of us to trundle ourselves, our gear, and our families sometimes halfway across the country in hopes of winning another ribbon. It all will all have been decided beforehand.

Honesty and courage of convictions

Regardless of how accurate you are when it comes to making evaluations or how logical and fair you are in making your decisions, unless you can be honest and courageous, you will never be able to really succeed in purebred dogs. This applies to both breeder and anyone operating in an official capacity in the show ring.

Breeders must be honest with themselves and with the people who come to them seeking help, advice, and breeding stock. Fixing bites and dyeing and faking of show stock can have serious repercussions with our governing kennel clubs. More lamentable, however, is that this form of deceit perpetuates faults in the breed you have dedicated yourself to improving. Certainly, this is in conflict with what a sincere breeder alleges to be his or her ultimate goal.

Licensed judges are no less (perhaps more?) responsible to the breeds they judge than are the breeders. The breeder as an individual usually shows but a few dogs in any given year, whereas a judge conceivably could pass upon a breed twenty or thirty times a year.

Intentionally awarding wins to dogs that are not in fact worthy of the recognition, or denying wins to dogs that deserve them, inflicts irreparable harm on a breed. Conduct of this kind is, without a doubt, the most serious fault a judge can have.

No one is beyond making a mistake. Nor is it impossible to add to one's understanding of a breed so that a person becomes better equipped to judge it. But out and out dishonesty or an inability to stand by what a judge believes to be correct is unforgivable. An "accommodating" judge wins many pats on the back and the derision of the people who really know their dogs.

Character and ability

Courage is an element of honesty, and together they represent a large part of character. Character stands equally alongside of ability in the characteristics of an outstanding dog person. In my eyes, there is nothing more deserving of scorn than the judge who has knowledge and ability but betrays it by being dishonest or accommodating. I am far more forgiving of the individual who does not know something and makes errors but is honest and tries to do a good job. I was told once, long ago, that the worst any honest man can do is make an honest mistake. I live by that motto.

The judge's job is never an easy one. No one has ever said it was, except those who have never tried their hand at it. There can be no considerations that come into play in a judge's mind other than the dog being presented at that very moment in time. What has happened before or what might yet happen must never be taken into account. The biggest or the smallest records, the most cleverly devised promotional campaign, or the entire absence of same, must have no consequence here.

The fact that a dog has won every show in sight without exception has no bearing on what a judge decides at the moment that dog is in the ring. Nor can the judge's like or dislike of the owner or handler of the dog come into play. Some exhibitors are extremely abrasive, others delightfully pleasant. This has absolutely nothing to do with the judge's evaluation of a dog, and a judge should never allow opinions regarding ownership or even pedigree to influence the decision.

Breeder judges often err in their decisions because they believe they have knowledge of some fault in a given dog's pedigree or in what a given dog produces. This does not have any place in judging dogs. This statement may prove distasteful to breeders, but judges may not penalize a dog for something they believe to be so. The fault is either there, observable and provable, or it is not. Second-guessing can lead to some very serious mistakes.

Prejudicial conduct

The same applies to judging the character of the exhibitor showing a dog. If the person on the end of the lead is guilty of prejudicial conduct, in the judges' ring, the person should be dismissed from the ring, or the officiating representative must be called should further action prove necessary. Allowing the guilty party to remain in the ring and placing the dog last or out of the ribbons does not correct the situation; it only follows one bad act with another.

On the other hand, as much as a judge might dislike an exhibitor for what has transpired outside of the ring, the judge must concentrate on the dog. Exhibitors are not paying their entry fees to have the judges fall in love with them, only to honestly evaluate their dogs.

There is often much pressure placed on a judge: pressure to put up a dog, pressure to put down the winning dog. Only those who can rise above situations such as these are in fact worthy of holding a license to judge.

Can a judge bend occasionally and allow ulterior considerations or motives to interfere with a decision? Once it starts, it never ends, and most judges who fall into that trap find they are compensating for past "favors" for all time to come. Once exhibitors note decisions of this kind, that judge will remain forever suspect.

Here I might add that a judge should never be so naive as to think no one will notice that favors have been done or unjust decisions made. There has never been a dog show held where competitors paid no attention to what a judge had done.

Roadblocks

Do I believe that most judges are honest and courageous? In general, I believe they are. I do, however, think that there is more to honesty and courage than meets the eye. There are many things that can interfere with an individual's putting honesty and courage into practice.

An indecisive person does not suddenly take on a new persona upon entering the show ring. People who have difficulty making up their minds can be as honest as the day is long, but they are easy targets for outside influences. Such a judge may believe dog "A" to be best, but this can be overshadowed by everyone else believing that dog "B" is the better of the two. It then becomes extremely difficult, if not impossible, for the indecisive person to go ahead and award dog "A" the prize, knowing the majority of opinion might disapprove.

Individuals who have ego problems can easily fall prey to making decisions that are not entirely honest. It would not be the least bit unusual for a person who feels inferior for whatever reason to use the show ring to exercise a level of superiority and show exhibitors "just who is boss" or give them "a taste of their own medicine."

As much as anyone might be tempted to give an exhibitor his or her "comeuppance" (deserved or otherwise), these are not honest decisions and have no place in the show ring. Judges who preside in this manner can easily fall prey to being what is often referred to as a "giant-killer" among judges and exhibitors. Giant-killers make every attempt to put down the top winner just to prove they can.

Advertising and its effects

Does advertising influence a judge's opinion? If I were to say no, I wouldn't be completely honest. Corporations do not spend billions of dollars on advertising annually just for the fun of it. Advertising is effective. I am not saying all advertising has a positive influence, but influence it does have.

Advertising is directed at affecting a person's opinion, and whether you want to believe it or not, beneath the judge's steely exterior there lies a person. Now, how someone goes about advertising his or her dogs and how it affects that person is another matter. Some individuals are extremely adept at presenting their dogs in a manner that gives all readers, including judges, a pleasant feeling. After reading the advertisement, one comes away with a positive feeling of some kind: the dog is cute, the dog is attractive, the dog is successful, and the owner feels appreciative.

Some advertising, unfortunately, makes such outrageous claims or predictions that it insults the reader's intelligence. It leaves a lingering bad taste with the person who has read the advertising copy.

Should this affect the judge's opinion of the dog in the ring? Absolutely not.

But does it? Only the judges themselves can tell you that. All I can say is that in dealing with judges, you are dealing with human beings, and I would feel much better about my chances if I were going into the ring with a positive image rather than a negative one. And that applies even if I know the judge is as honest as the day is long and possesses a level of integrity as high as Mt. Everest.

Why? Simply because there are many, many situations in which the differences between two quality dogs so balance out that it is almost impossible to make one's ultimate decision based on quality alone. The win might conceivably go to either of the dogs, and the judge would be entirely right.

In a situation like that, I would certainly prefer to be hanging onto the lead of a dog with a positive image than one whose reputation was associated with anything at all negative. I think you can understand the point I make.

Sound reasons

There is a critically interdependent relationship that exists between standard, breeder, and judge. Breed progress, or even breed maintenance, depends heavily upon excellence in all three of these areas.

The best breed standard in the world has no value if there aren't conscientious breeders actively doing their best to translate the standard's requirements into living, breathing dogs. And, in the end, someone must be available to determine whether these interpretations are valid ones. The person given this responsibility is the judge, who checks to see that trends in the breed do not exceed or fall below what the standard dictates.

An ability to have good reasons becomes a judging and evaluating essential because it assists in maintaining the standard-breeder-judge relationship that we could easily call "the breed progress triad." This ability has its foundation in an in-depth understanding of the breed standard. When an evaluator has sound reasons for decisions, it assists the breeder in living up to the requirements of that standard. This also gives evaluators a basis upon which to measure the validity of their placements and opinions.

It should be understood that correct decisions and correct placements can be made without giving any verbal reason for having done so. In fact, the American Kennel Club (AKC) recommends not doing so. While it is understandable why the AKC might prefer that a judge not do so, never knowing "why" does deprive the exhibitor of a learning experience. Even when no reasons are verbalized, the person doing the evaluating is not relieved of having sound reasons for making decisions.

How good reasons assist the judge

There are many different subjective influences in judging. However, whim or personal likes and dislikes should never be the overriding basis upon which judging decisions are made.

Dog fanciers eventually come to realize that a good breed standard asks for many things—far more than any one dog will ever have. A dog that excels in every characteristic of the standard would certainly have to be considered the first perfect dog; and just in case you haven't noticed, in dealing with dog breeding, there is no such thing as perfection.

It goes without saying that a given show dog might well possess what constitutes the "essence" of a breed. The dog may also embody far more of the ideal characteristics of a breed than another dog. But a dog that has everything—in the correct amounts and in the correct places? I seriously doubt any of us will live to see that happen.

Therefore, it becomes the judge's responsibility to be clear not only on what a standard demands but also on what a shortcoming really means in the overall picture. Often this will require a good amount of research into the history and origin of a breed. Let's use coat as an example.

There are some breeds in which a relatively healthy, at least somewhat typical coat is all a dog needs in order to comply with the breed standard. We might look to the Bull and Terrier breeds as an example. Straight forward, flat coats, no undercoat, and not much to be concerned about in the matter of texture.

On the other hand, amount and texture of coat as well as its distribution can be of paramount importance in other breeds. In fact, these factors can constitute a great part of what is considered the essence of a breed. We might use the Siberian Husky as an example here.

The Siberian is a dog of Nordic descent. The Nordic dogs were bred to be able to brave the rigors of the coldest winters and severest snow storms. Correct coat texture and where it should be most abundant became key survival factors.

In their homeland these dogs of the north had to have an outer coat that was straight and hard to shed rather than hold snow. This outer coat had to serve as a buffer against the winds and freezing temperatures of winter. It was important for the coat to be especially abundant, forming a mane around the neck and chest of the dog because that is where the vital organs are housed. The Nordic dog's undercoat had to be soft, thick, and insulating to keep body heat in.

Sound reasons assist the evaluation process by allowing proper weight to be placed on the degree a shortcoming departs from what is desired. Coat texture and amount have little bearing on the evaluation of a Bull Terrier as long as the coat is healthy. On the other hand, these same characteristics play a vital role in evaluating breeds of Nordic descent. Although the Siberian Husky standard does not go into great detail in this respect, it becomes both breeders' and judges' responsibility to give full attention to the breed's origin and purpose and act accordingly. Pictured is Siberian Husky Ch. Innisfree Sierra Cinnar, bred and owned by Kathleen Kanzler. (Ashbey photo)

Certainly it should be easy to see why it would not be possible to consider any Siberian Husky a quality example of its breed if the dog did not carry the kind of coat the breed standard and the breed's origin require. The Siberian standard does not go into great detail about the reasons for the breed's coat. This is information that must be researched and becomes part of the breeder's and the judge's knowledge of a breed. It gives the evaluator sound reasons for making important decisions.

Here again, even though a judge is not required to reveal a reason for making a final decision on this important aspect of a breed, there can certainly be no doubt as to how valuable this information is. This is especially so for those who are not yet educated enough to have made the observation on their own.

I read an article recently in which the author stated that "a fault is a fault" and should be penalized to the same extent, no matter what the breed.

That is a statement I would never be able to agree with. A poor coat on a Bull Terrier is what I would consider a failing—something I am not pleased with, but both the dog and I could live with. A poor coat in a breed where a specific type of coat was developed to keep the breed alive is an entirely different situation. Here a severe penalty is in order.

Unfortunately, many judges and longtime breeders fear making their reasons known (giving critiques) because it might offend someone. Critiques never have to be done in the negative. A critique can be entirely positive. There should be definite reasons why a dog is given a ribbon. If the dog has no merit to point out, no ribbon should be awarded. It's just about as simple as that.

How good reasons assist the breeder/exhibitor

No one shows to lose. It would be foolish to think anyone does. At the same time, if an exhibitor believes the only valid opinion is the one that agrees with his or her own, that is more than just a bit narrow-minded. When a judge does not give a dog the placement an exhibitor might like to have, or when a breed expert doesn't render as glowing an evaluation as the exhibitor hoped for, there is always disappointment. That is just human nature.

If the exhibitor is serious about making a contribution to the breed, however, or even if the only goal is to show a winning dog, what point is there in encouraging the person to remain on the wrong track? Is this being honest?

A true tale

This story, which I have told before but merits repetition here, relates to this very subject:

> Many years ago, a friend of mine was judging at a show in an out-of-the-way part of the country. As she was preparing to judge her next breed, she looked outside the ring and saw the Airedale Terrier that was the sole entry in that breed.
>
> She watched the dog and could tell the owner loved her dog as much as the dog loved her. They were the poster team for "man's best friend," as good a relationship between human and dog as could be asked for.
>
> There was just one problem. The dog was a terrible example of its breed! So poor, in fact, the judge wondered whether the dog was entirely purebred. Further, she realized that to award the dog anything at all would automatically make it Best Of Breed, and the dog would then have to go on to represent the breed in Terrier Group competition that night.
>
> As the exhibitor gazed down at her dog with love and pride, my friend the judge realized what it was she had to do. "Ma'am," she said, "I can see how much you care for your dog and how much he loves you. He must be a wonderful companion. It appears the two of you have a great relationship. Unfortunately, as far as the qualities needed for the show ring," she went on, "this dog really does not have enough of the characteristics needed to make him a dog of show quality.
>
> "I think the two of you would probably do wonderfully well in the Obedience ring, where intelligence and rapport are prime factors. And if you want to compete in the conformation ring, I would

suggest you look for a dog that conforms more closely to the standard of the breed."

The dog's owner thanked my friend most graciously, and with a tear in her eye and her arm around her dog's neck, she left the ring.

Postscript

Many years were to pass before my friend judged Best in Show at a very important show in the Midwest. Her choice for the top award was a beautiful Scottish Terrier female, and as pictures were being taken afterward, the owner-handler of the little Scottie said, "I know you won't remember me, but many years ago I showed an Airedale Terrier under you, and you withheld the ribbon. You advised me to show him in Obedience and to look for a better dog to show in conformation.

"Well, no one would sell me a good Airedale, so I decided to breed Scotties. This little bitch is the third consecutive generation of my breeding program. I am very proud of her and very thankful to you for giving me the advice you did."

As in life outside of dog shows, it is not always easy to tell the truth, but it must be told. We certainly do not want to discourage the newcomer from joining us in this game that we all play so enthusiastically, but on the other hand, why encourage someone to follow a path that leads nowhere? Wouldn't we be kinder to help set the novice in the right direction?

If the exhibitor or the breeder is given sound reasons for an evaluation that is less than flattering, it may put a bit of a dent in the person's ego, but what if your honesty creates a better breeder or helps an avid competitor reach the top?

Aren't you making a greater contribution in your capacity by telling the exhibitor who lost why she lost rather than leaving it to speculation and misunderstanding? Who is apt to learn more: the exhibitor who is told where her dog's problems lie, or the fellow who leaves the ring believing he lost because you are a better friend of the owner of the dog you put up?

Whether your good reasons are passed along to the person for whom they will do the most good or kept as your own private storehouse of knowledge, the bottom line is that they are important to have.

2 | Pictures on a Wall

Although there is little difference in what the breeder and the judge do, in today's dog game, oddly enough, judges derive far more recognition and certainly far more publicity than the breeder. The judge walks into the Best in Show ring wearing a stern expression and, if female, some four-figure Versace number. She scrutinizes the seven, usually high-quality, dogs and points to one of them.

The winning exhibitor does everything possible not to throw his arms around the judge in gratitude. Many pictures are taken, the judge signs the back of the Best in Show rosette, and she is whisked off to the bistro of the moment, where she's interviewed and complimented on every little gesture made in the preceding finals.

The breeder of the dog goes home.

Realistically, there would be no need for judges at all if we were to somehow lose our breeders. Nevertheless, the duties of both are so similar and so closely interrelated that making one more important than the other doesn't seem to make a great deal of sense.

In fact, I think we've lost sight of this relationship and see the two roles—breeder and judge—as distinct from one another, having separate goals.

I read somewhere that dog shows now are not so much to select breeding stock but more a social event, and that we should readjust our thinking to reflect this change.

Hogwash!

This isn't to say we don't have those in our midst who are here for a pleasant diversion. It goes without saying that they are present and more than welcome. However, it's not our responsibility or purpose as breeders and judges to entertain our Sunday visitors. We have a far more important job, and if a breeder or judge feels we are simply part of some social event, I shudder to think of the damage such thinking could create.

I've done a great deal of reading in my days in dogs. The walls of my office are lined with shelves filled with books written by brilliant dog men and women of the past century and beyond. Practically all of them see the roles of breeder and judge working in tandem, but nothing I've read captures the essence of this breeder-judge relationship I'm talking about more brilliantly than a few simple words written by the late breeder, handler, and judge Percy Roberts.

Roberts was a brilliant dog man born in England in the late 1800s. He bred dogs for himself, and he managed several of England's foremost breeding kennels. He later became a professional handler, working both in his home country and in the United States. When Roberts retired from handling, he went on to become a judge of all breeds in the United States and officiated at some of the world's most important shows. His prowess as breeder, handler, and judge earned him a reputation as one of the world's most brilliant dog men.

Roberts was often called upon to write for various publications, and on one occasion he wrote a piece that appeared in one of the popular dog publications of his time. The piece contained two lines that should guide the hand and mind of everyone who has an interest in purebred dogs.

The "Breed Progress Triad"

Roberts wrote, "A breed standard is the blueprint. The breeder is the builder and the judge is the building inspector."

Exactly when and where Roberts wrote these compelling words first has been lost in the passing of time. They were handed to me on a scrap of paper many years ago by a friend, with a note that indicated they had been written many years before that. They are as applicable today as they were the day they were written, and I suspect will remain so as long as purebred dog breeding holds the attention of humankind.

There is nothing I've read anywhere else, in articles or books, that contains more universal truth as applied to breeding and judging of quality purebred dogs than Roberts's simple analogy. He not only points out individual responsibilities with perfect clarity, he also reminds us just how interrelated and interdependent the standard, the breeder, and the judge really are. It is through this symbiotic relationship that the great dogs of yesterday were produced, and it is from this same relationship that the great dogs of tomorrow will be bred.

The dog game has grown since Roberts's day. It continually develops in size and sophistication. Now, many exhibit only for the fun of it. For them, it's simply a pleasant pastime.

That doesn't relieve us of our responsibility as breeders and judges. In fact, it imposes an even greater obligation on those of us who profess inclusion in either of these categories.

It's not really the responsibility of those who show "Honey" or "Brutus" or "Lassie" on an occasional Sunday to worry about preservation of breed type. However, without ongoing concern in this respect, the dog game as we know it will cease to exist. Someone must be concerned, and that "someone," it should come as no surprise, is anyone who claims to be a dedicated dog breeder or judge.

Selecting the proper tools

I think most people who undertake these roles are serious about what they do and well-meaning in how they go about doing it. Unfortunately, the tools employed to accomplish the job are not always those that can get the job done.

Roberts's "builder" wouldn't grab a saw to hammer nails, and those of us who breed or judge have to be extremely careful in selecting or recommending the tools to use in accomplishing a given end.

Let me give you an example.

Not too long ago, during a judging assignment, I was taking a break between classes and couldn't help but overhear the conversation between what apparently was a well-experienced Doberman breeder-exhibitor and a very intelligent-sounding but inexperienced novice. The breeder was doing her best to explain points of the breed standard to the beginner and was using the dog at the end of her lead as an example of what was correct.

The explanation was sound, accurate, and based on the many scientific principles now used to explain what a quality specimen of a dog breed should be. I was more than impressed with the breeder's extensive knowledge of anatomy and could tell the listener was just as impressed as I was—probably even more so, if the rapt attention he was giving his mentor was any indication.

The dog being used as a model had the bits and pieces of anatomy that were being explained. With no x-ray machine at hand, an observer could only assume the dog had all the requisite bones, and they appeared to be in approximately the proper places. The dog seemed to bear at least most of the proportions and relationships being discussed.

A job well done—or so it would seem.

In spite of the excellent explanation, the dog being used as an example was on his best day hardly able to qualify as anything more than "adequate."

Seeing is believing

I guess the situation bothered me more than it might someone else because of the way I learn. I am a visual learner and find many others I've taught are, as well. You can give me a dozen books and a dozen more audiotapes, and I will hope to get at least an idea of what you're trying to get across. Unfortunately, the more intricate details there are to contend with, the less apt I am to get the entire picture.

However, show me one example of exactly what you want me to know, and I'll burn that image into my mind so that I will recognize it instantly the next time I see it. That fixed image also allows me to recognize where a subject strays from the ideal.

I'm one of those people who'd find it much easier to handle those "some assembly required" directions much better if I could see someone else do it first or see illustrations of what is meant by "attach-part-A-to-part-C-through-the-loophole-in-part-B." Text-only directions are apt to result in my efforts resembling an ironing board rather than the computer desk that was intended.

Written standards are all well and good, and I'll eventually get the picture the written words attempt to impart; but show me a living, breathing example of what the standard is aiming at, and that picture clicks in and remains with me until I consciously choose to retouch it.

I've seen and judged a good many Flat Coat Retrievers in my day and can only assume that not having been burned at the stake thus far for my decisions, I've been at least somewhere near on target. That is, I've been able to sort the good ones from the bad ones and put up at least one of the good ones.

But then one day, at an uncelebrated show in the middle of the country, a young bitch in the minor classes walked into my ring who embodied in one presence all the best words, pictures, and parts of all the other Flat Coats I had previously seen. The young bitch proved beyond a shadow of a doubt that what *should* be was also possible.

All I want to see is "the good one." Don't confuse the issue with eighty-eight examples of what is *not* wanted.

Please understand, I'm not discounting research and study. That's what prepares you to be able to recognize the great one when it walks into your ring or appears in your whelping box. But what brings all those parts and pieces and well-written books into focus is seeing *in the flesh* what all the theory is about.

It was Anne Rogers Clark who so succinctly put this all into perspective for me one afternoon many years ago. We were all sitting around talking dogs in the penthouse of the Hyatt Regency in Atlanta, Georgia. It was over the *Kennel Review* Tournament of Champions weekend, and there were plenty of outstanding breed examples to refer to and to be talked about. Mrs. Clark, her late husband, Jim, and a few others of us were talking about "getting it": that moment of epiphany one has when all the parts and pieces come together, and what was purely academic becomes real and concrete.

Mrs. Clark talked about one dog in particular and said something to the effect that the dog was the kind that helped her to create her "breed template." I hadn't heard the term used before, and I asked what she meant.

She responded that it was that picture created by the "right" dog, the dog who has it all, who pulls all the pieces, all the reading, and all the conversation together and stamps out a silhouette in a permanent mental template through which all subsequent dogs of that breed are viewed.

"Brilliant," I thought at the time, and I see it that way to this day.

Returning to our Doberman ringside scenario....

Developing the picture

While the breeder was giving her speech in respect to what the breed standard requires, the novice was taking in every word, but more importantly, he was taking a mental picture—and interpreting what was being said on the basis of what stood before him.

I have to be honest and say the dog at hand might have been in total compliance with the principles governing what a sound Doberman Pinscher should be capable of doing. The only problem was that he wasn't a particularly good Doberman!

Even if the breeder had been astute enough to say, "this dog is not exactly what we are after," the picture was still being taken—the template being created and the harm being done. While I can't speak with any certainty as to what the novice went away with, I can't help but expect him to have been interpreting the explanation in terms of what he was seeing.

It is easiest for most people to learn visually. Using the best example of what is wanted avoids clutter and confusion and helps to stamp the image of what is correct in the learner's mind. This portrait of Mr. & Mrs. Sam Lawrence's Ch. Brunswig's Cryptonite is far more apt to convey the message most Doberman Pinscher evaluators want understood than one in which shortcomings have to be explained away. It's the entire picture that makes the great dog. Granted, the dog must have all those parts, but none of them are of consequence if they don't add up to the desired whole. (Don Petrulis photo)

This is my opinion, and I'm more than happy to own it lock, stock, and barrel, but I do not believe it is scientific principles that create our great dogs. There's no denying that our rare greats have those parts and that those parts work in a fashion that makes our engineers wax ecstatic, but it's not quite as simple as that.

It's the entire picture that makes the great one, and although a dog's designation as such comes through having all or most of those *parts*, it is the dog's unique ability to unite and operate them all correctly that elevates it to a level of distinction.

There has been more than one dog whose parts earned high marks but who failed as a complete specimen. I referred to Ch. Rock Falls Colonel as being "a successful sum of all the parts." The operative word here is "sum" rather than "parts." If you can make that distinction in the dogs you observe, it will help you tremendously in understanding why some dogs are said to possess great type while others are not. The following chapters will explain why.

I'm aware that what I say in this respect inspires my more scientifically prone comrades to take up scholarly arms in defense of their position, but I'll stand by my tattered banner of opinion until the last battle has been fought.

Actually, I am *pleased* that what I believe creates discussion. There's so much follow-the-leaderism (if there is such a term!) in today's dog game that I live in constant fear that someone up at the front of the line will suddenly stop one day, and we'll have a collision of such catastrophic proportions that the dog game will never recover!

When I hit a nerve that inspires reaction, I'm thrilled. It proves we still have living, breathing, and thinking dog men and women out there who do more than allow themselves to be carried along by the winds of fad and fancy.

Does it bother me that I am challenged on statements I've made questioning the *Popular Mechanics* approach to evaluating dogs? Not at all. As far as I'm concerned, *any* discussion that is even remotely linked to the importance of breed type, pro or con, is a step in the right direction.

Do I discount the advances science has made that enable us to understand how and why our dogs do what they do? Of course not. But I see appreciation and recognition of type as something far more basic and essential—a prerequisite, if you will—for anyone who really hopes to make contributions as a breeder or judge. And that appreciation comes from exposure and comparison—in the end, from a recognition of line, balance, symmetry, subtlety, and the many other artistic qualities that produce a work of art. There may not be scientific terms, but certainly there are bottom-line essentials in both judging and breeding.

Honing and developing our ability in this area allows us to recognize the essence of what makes each and every breed distinct, and the greater our ability to do so, the more apt we are to appreciate high excellence when it appears.

What I've dubbed as the Popular Mechanics *approach to evaluation has us concentrate on what each of the individual parts of a dog does rather than having us keep the whole in mind. The image projected by most Sporting Dogs and many other breeds is one in which one part flows freely, subtly into the next, with no jarring or abrupt angles. This picture of Cocker Spaniel Ch. Beau Monde More Paint, bred by the author and Darla Piner, clearly illustrates this principle. More Paint is handled here by Don Johnston with judge Rosalie Anderson. (Pegini photo)*

A prehistoric art

Humankind has had the ability to employ balance, symmetry, and proportion far longer than most would ever have imagined. Discovery of the Chauvet Cave art in France in 1994 revealed that only a few thousand years after the first anatomically modern humans appeared in Europe, we were making ingenious use of elegant lines, perspective, and subtle shading. Our ability to do so produced images on the cave walls that portrayed the animal kingdom that existed at that time.

Carbon dating has revealed these images were created some 35,000 calendar years ago! There is no difficulty in recognizing the intent of the cave artists because they captured the very essence of each and every one of the animals portrayed. In fact, these artists had such a clear concept of what was important to each of the animals they portrayed and had such a marvelous sense of perspective that they were able to accurately project these images on a panel stretching some thirty feet across. This was in spite of the fact that they were only able to step a few feet back from the wall due to the narrow limitations of the cave itself.

It's about vision of the whole—the essence of the subject!

If you want to get the most out of what you will read and see in the coming chapters of this book, I ask that you put away your slide rules, compasses, and engineering primers. After you have finished reading what I have written, you will then be free to get back to the drafting table, but bear with me for the course of this book.

If you do so, I think you'll find you've added tremendously to your understanding of what breed type is really all about, and you just may find out how little that knowledge conflicts with the scientific principles you may already have embraced or will embrace in the future.

If it were entirely up to me, I wouldn't permit any student of mine to go anywhere near a T-square, ruler, or compass in the initial stages of learning a breed. After thorough saturation with excellence repeated often enough to be able to recognize it easily—only when the subtleties that create the difference between good and great became apparent—then and only then would I allow them to pick up their drafting equipment.

First the whole

A few years back I participated in a parent club Judges Breed Study group. First thing in the morning, the aspiring judges were whisked off to a room where they were inundated with charts, graphs, and measuring tapes. They were given an explanation of how to measure every bone from nose to toes. When the judges-to-be emerged from the lecture, their eyeballs were spinning.

It was my assignment to take over next—to do the ringside mentoring while the regular classes of the show were being judged. The individuals in the group who were at least beginning to come out of the morning's mind-boggler began asking questions.

"What percentage do you allow for length of the pastern when compared to the entire length of the bones of the forehand assembly?" "Should we attempt to get the dogs to canter in the ring to see if there are in fact three beats to every stride?" *And those were the simple questions!*

The first thing I told them was that I didn't have a clue! The second thing was to hold all those questions for a Frank Lloyd Wright introductory course, and put all the graphs and charts they were given under their seats. For now, we were just going to look at some dogs and attempt to pick out the good ones.

As the regular classes came and went, I called my students' attention to the dogs whose silhouettes represented the ideal or close to it, the dogs whose height at the withers were in proper proportion to their length of body.

I pointed out the dogs that had the right balance and the right length of neck, making sure they understood how important that was. The breed at hand was one in which upright shoulder optically cuts down on length of neck and adds to length of back, but at that point my object was having them identify what was right. *Why it was right would come later.* I had them concentrate only on the dogs that had what we were looking for and told them to burn those images into their minds.

When I sensed they were recognizing the desired overall silhouette, only then did I begin to turn their attention to what represented the desired head and expression in the breed. I just pointed out the dogs that had the "look" that typified the breed. After pointing out a number of examples, I had the student judges identify the dogs that they thought had what was needed in the head department.

It wasn't long before they were beginning to get it and began separating the wheat from the chaff on their own. By the time we went through movement and the Specials had come parading in, most of the students were making the same cuts our judge (a very good judge, I might add) was making.

Outcome

Since that time I've had the opportunity to sit ringside and watch some of those people who were students back then and who are now at work as full-fledged judges. The ones I've observed have done very creditable jobs.

Do I always agree their decisions? No. But that's not the point. They have the essence of the breed down and know how to separate the dogs, making the right picture right from the get go. Right off the bat, they pull out the dogs that portray the breed best and then start looking into the details to make more fine-line decisions.

Here again, balance and flow aided by smooth transitions result in the exceptional whole of Ch. Tal-E-Ho's Top Banana, a Basset Hound considered by many to be one of the finest the breed has produced. Top Banana was owned by Peter and Bryan Martin and is pictured here winning the Basset Hound Club of America National Specialty under Mrs. Frances Messinger. (Booth photo)

They've obviously added to their knowledge since that day at ringside and have probably been coached on the mechanics responsible for why some of those dogs can and can't do what the standard dictates. But more importantly, they are able to instantly recognize the dogs in the lineup that *are the breed*.

As an educator I would want my people to recognize a good one first *and then* go on to find out what the parts and pieces, angles, or lack of them mean and how they work. As a breeder and student, I need more of that than I do endless dialogues on parts and pieces.

Why?

Because I find that developing, honing, and trusting one's eye for quality makes better judges and better breeders than does isolating the parts and allowing the parts to take precedence over the whole.

Do the rules of kinesiology, biomechanics, and engineering have bearing on our study of purebred animals? Of course!

However, we do not enter the show ring or look into the whelping box looking for proof of our formulas. We look there to find that animal with that unquestionable stamp of quality—who portrays the essence of the breed.

This applies to breeding as well as it does to judging.

Magic formulas

Only recently, I attended an excellent seminar in which the lecturer had devised some very impressive formulas and equations for successful dog breeding. They were based on genetic research and scientific principles. As the gentleman worked out the formulas on the blackboard, I heard little gasps of delight as those in attendance began to understand what the formulas meant.

During a break I had coffee with a number of rather successful longtime breeders who had attended. I found most of them were delighted to find that the scientifically calculated formulas confirmed the practices they had been employing over the years. As one old gal, a breeder of many famous champions, added jokingly, "Glad to hear I haven't been doing it wrong all these years."

There was a lot to be learned that day. I found it well worth the time and came away with a good deal to think about, as did the other experienced breeders who had attended.

The disappointing part of the occasion came at the seminar's conclusion. I couldn't help but overhear the conversations of some of the day's participants. It was clear our lecturer had made the points he set forth very well and had convinced his audience of the value of his formulas.

Unfortunately, the point that he did not stress nearly enough was that the formulas for success were entirely dependent upon the user's thorough understanding of correct type in his or her breed. Then and only then would the user be able to effectively bring together the right elements of those equations that would allow them to work.

That those prerequisites had been too readily assumed by the speaker and not stressed enough became more and more apparent as I heard the participants marvel at how much time they had wasted doing this, that, and the other thing, in order to breed good dogs. Their take was that successful dog breeding was much simpler than they had made it—that success was easily achievable by using the magic formulas and equations.

As I walked off to my car, I couldn't help but think, only in their dreams. Obviously, my fellow students were under the mistaken assumption that the ends were totally the result of the means—that the formulas did the work, not the dogs brought together for use *in* the formulas.

Science is an adjunct to a breeding program, and it is generous to those who use it in conjunction with a crystal-clear picture of the ultimate goal. It's a whole lot easier to put the right parts together when you know what the end result should be. That's not any kind of genius—it's good old cave-man sense.

3 | Eliminating the Confusion

*I*f you were given a single dollar for every time someone broached the subject of breed type in the last decade, you'd be well on your way to a place among the rich and famous. If we could somehow calculate how many times the term will be discussed in even the next couple decades and pay you for that—well, if that were the case you probably wouldn't be reading this at all. You'd be off on that trip to Tahiti, embarking on your goal to play the great golf courses of the world, or cooling your heels in your villa overlooking the Mediterranean—all the while chuckling over how you used to spend time arguing about what breed type was or wasn't and the dogs that did and didn't have it.

There is no doubt about it. If I were going to compile a list of buzz words for the dog game, breed type would most certainly have to head that list.

It makes no difference where you fall on the dog fancy's scale of involvement or what's being discussed—sooner or later, the conversation will turn itself to the two words that describe the most important term in the dog fancier's lexicon. And, if you retained anything at all from the previous chapters, it would have to be the fact that we've become pretty adept at creating clouds to obscure what the term is really all about.

It appears that ever since dog shows got under way in earnest, those two little words with the great big meaning have been explained, discounted, pitted against, dismissed, and revered. It seems coming up with any kind of answers to the questions those words inspire is an exercise in futility.

For instance, there's that age-old conundrum involving type that evidently has eternal life. You know—the one that starts off with, "Which is more important, type or soundness?"

That one generates enough heat to solve the energy problems of the Isle of Manhattan. The question has been dealt with periodically and pretty conclusively by some pretty savvy dog people around the world, and yet it seems to resurface time and time again.

Perhaps it's because the argument's participants don't want to admit that as far as dogs are concerned, the two terms don't stand in opposition and they don't stand alone. They work together. If there were a simple "one or the other" answer to the question, it would make life much easier for everyone involved—because getting one or the other is far easier than finding both to an acceptable degree in the same animal.

Still, it's hard to understand why, after all the explanations, the fact that type and soundness can't stand alone remains such a closely guarded secret. If I've read one perfectly logical explanation, I've read a couple dozen; and yet completely sincere and intelligent fanciers still keep asking *which* is more important.

As an example, I'll use a contribution that appeared in the "Bark Back/Sound Off" department of *Dogs In Review*. Basically, it's the section of that magazine where readers have an opportunity to write in their objections to an article or ask questions that they haven't been able to get answers to elsewhere.

One of those letters came from a concerned person who had recently judged the sweepstakes classes of a Specialty show for a particular breed. In the letter the writer spoke of "a bitch in a small class who was plain, not very typey (who) never put a foot wrong." It appears the writer was somewhat taken by this particular bitch despite the fact that "comments and opinions of the 'bystanding judging public' were adamant on type over soundness."

In order to make intelligent comments on the class referred to, we would really need to have seen the class. So much depends upon what all the dogs looked like on the day—how lacking in type the bitch in question was and to what degree the typey ones were unsound.

"On the day" is extremely important. I can remember saying years ago, before I started judging, that it would have been impossible to put such and such a dog over another of the same breed. Once I started judging, however, I realized that doing just that would be more than possible. The factors in judging are all far too variable to ever say *never*.

Yes, that flashy, "never puts a foot wrong" kind of a dog will have a place in the ribbons when there are no dogs there that both excel in breed type and are reasonably sound enough to place over it. But that is not what a judge is looking to do. Rewarding the dog whose *only* virtues are flash and soundness, over one of correct type that might be marred only by a degree of unsoundness, is counterproductive to what breeding show-quality animals is all about.

I will explain why.

Certainly you've seen that mixed-breed dog trotting down the street—head held high, level topline, tail waving happily behind him—glancing right and left as if he owned the world. His front legs reaching, the hindquarters driving, all in perfect balance and coordination. What else could you ask of a dog?

A lovely sight, right? Sound? Well, in a general sense, yes. He has all his proper parts in place and functioning as they should for a dog. It appears he can see, can hear, and has obviously been able to eat well enough to keep him in fine fettle.

But don't ask things like whether or not he is of proper size or if his attractive way of going is suitable for retrieving or galloping or for draught purposes. Don't get too technical, because the dog has no standard of quality against which to be judged. He has no criteria to meet. So he's sound (not infirm), and he's showy (a jolly temperament). Nothing more, nothing less.

Frankly, most successful breeders give away sound, showy dogs as pets year after year. They come from the deepest blue of blooded lines. If soundness and charisma were the ultimate criteria for selection, the breeder's task would be greatly simplified. But it is much more complicated than that for the breeder and for the judge.

What complicates the equation is that we're given the "type" factor to deal with. Type carries us into an entirely different arena and dictates a whole barrage of considerations. Instantly, it's not just that a dog is putting his feet down in a functional manner and moving along easily that is of consequence. Success comes only if he is doing so in the manner dictated by the breed's standard—and that based upon the breed's origin, purpose, and construction.

Nor will a jolly, tail-waving temperament necessarily be the criterion that defines correctness for the breed. And even if it were—the *degree* to which the dog exhibited that characteristic could well come into play.

It would only stand to reason that in order for a given purebred to embody the essence of its breed, it would most certainly have to reflect the *purpose* of that breed, whether that purpose were to be built strong enough to pull, fast enough to catch, or small enough to be carried around in someone's pocket.

We don't need or want our Saluki to be constructed so that it is able to bring down and hold a four-hundred-pound gorilla. Nor do we want our Pom to be constructed in a manner suitable to streaking off across the desert after some leopard. What we are looking for is *appropriate* soundness.

*Purpose dictates soundness, and that is determined by the standard of the breed and by the breed's origin and purpose. Soundness in Saluki terms is expressed in an ability to move with speed, flexibility, and endurance. Generally speaking, the Saluki performed over desert sands, so the breed had to be light of body to propel itself **over** rather than into the ground beneath its feet. George and Sally Bell's Ch. Bel S'mbran Promise of Attalah exhibits all the named characteristics and presents a picture of an animal capable of functioning in the manner described. Promise is pictured here winning Best in Show under judge Mrs. Keke Khan. (Vicky Cook photo)*

*The Pom's role is that of an easily handled companion. There is no need or excuse to choose the Pom that is deformed or handicapped. However, care must be taken in interpreting the final lines of the breed standard, which state that the breed is "subject to the same requirements of soundness and structure prescribed for all breeds." The standard refers to the **principles governing** canine soundness and does not mean that its movement resembles that of a St. Bernard or Border Collie. Pictured is Ch. Coy's Top Of The Mark, whose construction and movement satisfied both the breed expert and all-rounder, carrying him to an outstanding show career. The Best in Show judge was Dr. Samuel Draper. Toddie Clark did the handling for owner Alan Novick. (Earl Graham photo)*

We want our breeds to look like what they were conceived to look like in the first place. And if they are constructed in that manner, we can only assume they will be able to perform in that manner, whether that's dashing off after the gorilla or slipping into your pocket.

You cannot put soundness in opposition to type. Separating soundness from type all too often leads to imposing the general rules of soundness on breeds not governed by them. For instance, the correct Miniature Pinscher moves with hackney motion in its forehand. Boxers have undershot jaws. The Chow Chow moves with a stilted gait, and the Pekingese has foreshortened and bowed front legs. These breeds are as their standards say they should be. They are appropriately sound because they are made as their standards require. It is important not to confuse breed soundness with efficiency.

*The properly constructed Pekingese has foreshortened and bowed front legs. Its gait described in the standard is "unhurried and dignified, with a slight roll over the shoulders." Reach, drive, and speed (qualities desirable in some breeds), would constitute a major fault in correct and therefore **sound** movement for a Peke.*

In these breeds, or in any purebred dog, for that matter, soundness is determined by type. The absence of soundness would constitute a serious blemish, but it is just as important to understand that the presence of generic soundness without the other factors that determine type is of little value to the breeder.

Following in the footsteps of my mentors, I evaluate any given dog on the basis of how much good is there: that is, how it excels in those basic components that make a breed distinctive. If there is a failing, I deal with the shortcoming much in the same way The Kennel Club of England's breed standards conclude—"in the exact proportion to its degree." This applies to the way the dog looks, the way it's constructed, and the way it moves.

Returning to the letter writer's concern, I would be inclined to say that despite the fact that soundness in the breed in question is desirable, rewarding the "plain, not very typey" bitch for soundness alone would ignore all else the breed standard calls for. It would be no different than ignoring an entire standard to put up the smallest dog in the ring because one line of that standard reads, "the smaller dog being an element of success." The smaller dog is in fact *an* element of success but not the *only* element of success.

There would be no purpose at all in writing a detailed standard, if in fact a member of the breed had only to qualify in one respect in order to be outstanding. Soundness, size, color—no *one* characteristic can possibly describe or define a breed. To evaluate the dog on the basis of one characteristic makes little sense. It dismisses the very purpose of a breed standard—to impart the total essence (in other words, type) of the breed.

*One of the most distinctive characteristics of the Miniature Pinscher is its "hackney-like gait in which the action is...high-stepping, reaching, free and easy...the front leg moves straight forward and in front of the body and the foot bends at the wrist." Although a well laid-back shoulder might present a more "attractive" picture in the MinPin outline, it's only **moderate** angulation there that will assist the required and highly distinctive movement. A straighter shoulder is thus correct **for the breed**. Demonstrating that required and therefore perfectly **sound** movement and construction is Ch. Dynasty's Speaking Of Him, owned by Helen C. Greene and Jack Chrysler. (Kitten Rodwell photo)*

A dangerous trend

But then, even if we are all in agreement that type is of consequence and it *includes* what some try to isolate, what about the all-too-popular opinion that there are many "types" within a breed? Personally, I feel that the word "types" in this instance is not only a misconception of the true meaning of type, it again misses the very purpose of breed standards.

This position represents a dangerous trend that could pose a serious threat to our pursuit of the ideal. We all know there are variations within any breed—dogs that fall to one side or the other of the ideal, the ideal being what most of us refer to as correct type.

I fear, however, that far too many are interpreting this accepted variance to mean that there is no true type: no bull's eye to aim for. They seem to believe that as long as an individual specimen has the general breed characteristics, has no disqualifying faults, and is basically sound, the dog in question is just as good as the rest being shown.

I've heard those supporting this "anything goes" school of thought point out that absolute consistency in type is only required in the wild, where natural selection is directly related to survival of the species. There, deviation from the required type, unless an improvement, threatens survival.

There can be no argument with nature's code. However, I find it impossible to accept that because our purebred dogs are artificially created, there is no need for us to be particularly strict in culling deviations because our decisions have nothing to do with survival—that what we do is all arbitrary to begin with.

Those who subscribe to this theory seem to believe uniformity is necessary only to the degree that it can distinguish one breed from all others. The resulting variation would then permit sufficient room for flexibility in determining what is acceptable.

How the advocates of this diversity think a breeder could set goals or a judge would ever be consistent in placements is beyond me. But perhaps that is the point—anything and everything would be fine and dandy.

Supporters of this theory are inclined to see believers in only one true type as prejudicial and incapable of appreciating other views. Prejudicial I might well be, but my considerable involvement with dogs has yet to find a breeding program based on the position that all's fair that has produced anything of consequence. Can you imagine how this might be received by those who for a lifetime have considered that the element of success rests in developing a line that enjoys familial similarity—one that requires no show catalog to determine the breeding? And consider the heretical thought this represents to someone who has spent a lifetime looking for the ideal specimen against which all subsequent members of a breed are compared.

I do not believe that "types" should be used to explain the variations that exist within a breed. Humans can't help but interpret a standard differently. We interpret everything we see through our own life experiences. However, there are limitations to how far we may carry our interpretations and still be correct.

"No two people see the same movie" is an old entertainment-industry axiom that can be applied equally to purebred dogs. For instance, not everyone is going to come away from a Woody Allen film with the same interpretation. Some see Allen as a comedic genius; others may not find his brand of humor particularly entertaining. That said, someone emerging from one of Allen's films crying buckets and saying the movie would be worthy of a musical score by Puccini just might have missed the point.

There is room for interpretation and expression in all things, but there are also limitations. A column written by Susan B. Lennard, the St. Bernard columnist for *AKC Gazette*, addresses these limitations and sheds defining light on the mistaken notion that there are different "types" within a given breed. Her piece was directed primarily at those interested in the St. Bernard, but it applies universally. I quote in part.

> "Type may be defined as the quality common to a specific group that distinguish the group as an identifiable class. Deviations from these qualities result in a loss of type. Our standard describes St. Bernard type.
>
> "Style, on the other hand, allows for latitude in the expression of the qualities that make up type. The extent of expression may contribute to or deviate from aspects of the phenotype described in our standard. Style may be an adjunct to type, but it is not the same thing. With this in mind it is important to evaluate style, why it exists and what impact it has on type.
>
> "Speculation as to what events surrounded the origin of our breed is left to your imagination. Written documentation serves as our only record. The Swiss standard was confirmed in 1887 and adopted in the U.S. in 1888. With its publication, we were presented with concrete guidelines with which

to assess our breed. Type was thereafter defined by the standard, which continues to guide us today.

"Yet it is difficult to chart the entire dog with its multitude of measurements and delineations. Herein lies an opportunity to express style. Structural differences may be observed through a study of morphometric measurements conducted in the late 1800s and early 1900s. Detailed measurements reveal deviations in proportions relating to head, body, length and height. Do we therefore exclude these areas from the definition of proper type because of the variations in proportion or might it be said that overall type remained while preferred values were assigned to symmetry and balance?

"We are now presented with a similar study as we view dogs from various areas of the country. There appear to be several styles inherent to specific regions. Some may argue that these differences are a result of conscious decisions to maintain individuality. I suggest it has more to do with concentrated gene pools than with individual expression. It is less expensive and certainly easier to use dogs within one's local area, and line-breeding produces greater consistency.

"Furthermore, style continues to exist to the extent that breeders isolate and correct the problems that are most important to them. One breeder focuses on improving qualities of the head, another concentrates on rears. The result is a difference in phenotype.

"However, we do not pursue style, we seek type. If viewed as a consequence in a never-ending process by which we achieve perfection, style may be viewed as a step toward progress. Only if it is used within the confines of our breed standard does it illustrate an attempt to produce better dogs. This should be our sole objective."

Ms. Lennard's analysis of type and style should hold a prominent place in the primer of every person who undertakes dog breeding or dog judging. If nothing else, her one line, *"However, we do not pursue style, we seek type,"* should be hung over every whelping box and at the entrance to every show ring in the country—because this is so often where we as breeders and judges stray. And she points out that style is only of value if it contributes toward achieving the ultimate goal; type is a profound guideline that should channel every step taken by a breeder.

Maintaining correct type in any of the giant breeds is a task equal to the size of these huge dogs. The St. Bernard is certainly no exception. However, type remains as important in this breed as it does in any purebred breed of dog. Many dog fanciers both new and experienced refer to variations from the ideal as a "different type" of dog. Are there different "types" within a breed, or does the standard establish what is correct for a breed? Former AKC St. Bernard columnist Susan B. Lennard addresses this age-old question in this chapter. Pictured is the all-breed Best in Show winner Ch. RRR's Super Samson, handled by James Berger for owners James & Georgia Rush. The judge was Mrs. Mary N. Stephenson. (Booth photo)

4 Defining the Term

*H*ayes Blake Hoyt was one of America's most respected and successful breeder-owner-handlers of the '30s, '40s, and '50s. She had an enormous record of accomplishments with her Poodles, including handling her own Standard Poodle, Int. Ch. Nunsoe Duc de la Terrace of Blakeen, to Best in Show at Westminster Kennel Club.

Mrs. Hoyt also enjoyed great respect throughout the world as a connoisseur of fine dogs of all breeds and as an award-winning dog writer. She was a regular columnist and contributor to *Kennel Review* for many of the years during which I was owner and publisher.

Many of Mrs. Hoyt's literary contributions concerning breed type have become classics in the annals of purebred dogs. One piece is particularly relevant to our discussion of the elusiveness of the term.

> "In dog parlance, one of the most misused words is 'type;' perhaps this is because many fanciers and even breeders interpret this word rather than define it. For instance, one breeder recently referred to type as 'moving correctly;' another wrote, 'type is elegance;' and a Poodle breeder and judge remarked, 'The blacks are always superior in type to whites.'... One can understand the bewilderment of the novice fancier of any breed, and particularly of our Poodle breed, over the simple statement, 'That dog has type.'"

It is important to understand why Mrs. Hoyt felt that our interpreting the word "type," rather than defining it, is what in a great part has contributed to the ongoing confusion. In order to have better focus on the point she makes, let's take a close look at the actual meaning of the two words.

INTERPRET (interpretation): 1) An individual's explanation of the meaning or intention of a written piece, a concept, a work of art; example—Helen's dogs are a fine interpretation of the characteristics called for in the breed standard. 2) To attribute a specific meaning to; example—he interprets the words "slightly longer" to mean no more than one inch.

DEFINE: 1) To state the precise meaning of; example—a dog's back is the dorsal surface [topline] commencing from the withers and ending at the loins/croup junction. 2) To be what characterizes something; example—the Great Dane is an example of what is known as a giant dog breed; 3) To describe precisely; example—the dog is eleven and three-quarters inches tall at the withers and fourteen inches long from point of shoulder to buttocks.

With a more clear-cut understanding of the words "interpret" and "define," let's take a look at another commonly used word in the dog person's vocabulary—opinion. Comparing "opinion" to "interpret" and "define" gives all three words even greater clarity.

OPINION: A mental estimate; a belief or conviction, based on what seems probable or true but not on demonstrable fact; example—"Of all the Collies I've known, Champion Winter Wonder is without a doubt the best."

The horse before the cart

My telling you Tom Brown's Collie, Winter Wonder, is the epitome of breed type tells you that I am using the dog as an interpretation of what I believe (opinion) to be outstanding breed type.

Let's assume you believe my word to be gospel truth. You might then take a picture of the dog in your mind's eye as we did in Chapter 2—this to create your mental template of the Collie breed. You do then in fact have an image to use when comparing other Collies to that picture. You now know what we are looking for in Collies, right? A first step well taken.

However, questions remain.

Do you understand why Winter Wonder represents ideal type? Will you be able to determine how much deviation in another Collie it would take to stray from what correct Collie type is? Has this picture you've created assisted you in any way in determining what correct breed type might be another breed?

On the basis of what has been presented here, I believe you would be hard pressed to give a positive response to these questions. At this point, my knowing Winter Wonder has breed type doesn't do you a whole lot of good beyond Winter Wonder. My interpretation and my opinion, as correct as they might be, don't make any headway in helping you to understand how I arrived at that decision.

All I've really established thus far is that, in my assumed expert opinion, Winter Wonder has outstanding breed type. Nothing I've said proves the point. I haven't made any attempt to define what criteria I use to establish whether this dog (or any dog, for that matter) has type.

This is not your fault, by any means—it's mine. I haven't passed along the tools I've used in arriving at my conclusion.

This scenario is typical of what transpires in the dog game day in and day out. We're told "that's it," but we never learn who made "it" it or why. This leaves us to decide on our own what in the standard puts a dog like Winter Wonder a notch or more above all others.

This is just an example of the main reason why so much interpreting and opinion giving goes on. It also puts us in touch with how few attempts are made at actually defining the whole issue of breed type.

I started thinking about the many famous dogs I've known through the years. It became apparent that some of them were a part of purebred dog history because of their achievements in the ring, yet others stood out not by merit of record alone but because of something special—something that had earned them pretty much across-the-board agreement that they enjoyed outstanding type.

The question that began to present itself was, what made both the Bulldog Ch. Westfield's Cunomorous Stone and the English Cocker Spaniel Ch. Dunelm Galaxy typey? The two breeds couldn't be more distant in what their standards asked for, but by and large, my contemporaries pretty well agreed that the two ranked very high on the breed type scale.

I began to thumb back through the pages of my memory to see what dogs in my past had been awarded this distinction over others that had not. It didn't take long to see that fame in itself had little to do with the determination. I did my best to be as objective as possible and used as much of my own knowledge as I could, but I also sought the opinion of other experienced people in the various breeds whose opinions I respected.

What I needed was a collection of dogs generally conceded to be of great type that I could take a serious look at, so I could see what it was they shared that might have set them apart from other dogs. Admittedly, I used ring achievements to some extent, but only to help identify the dogs, not to determine where they stood in respect to type.

The incomparable Bulldog bitch Ch. Westfield's Cunomorous Stone, handled by her breeder-owner to thirty-eight all-breed Bests in Show, twenty-four Specialty Bests in Show, and one hundred forty Non Sporting Group Firsts, an unequaled record in Bulldogs for her sex.

Chapter 4 Defining the Term 59

Richard Bauer campaigned Ruth Cooper's Ch. Dunelm Galaxy to a great show record, but there can be no doubt that his type has influenced the breed without measure. Galaxy sired ninety-three champions. His son Ch. Kenobo Rabbit sired fifty-five champions, and his grandson Ch. Kenobo Capricorn sired one hundred twenty champions. If any dog has ever earned the title "type setter," it is most certainly Ch. Dunelm Galaxy. (Rudolf Tauskey photo)

Wood Wornell campaigned Linda Honey's Irish Terrier, Ch. Rock Ledge Mac Michael, to noteworthy wins throughout the country, but it was the dog's ability to transmit his acclaimed breed type that created an entire renaissance for the breed. Michael is pictured here winning Best in Show under Langdon Skarda. (Gilbert photo)

60   Solving the Mysteries of Breed Type

Irish Setter Ch. McCammon's Marquis impressed Sporting Dog fans from Coast to Coast as a show dog and earned historic significance as the model upon which the Irish Setter Club of America's illustrated standard is based. He is pictured winning Best in Show under Michelle Billings. Marquis was handled by George Alston for owner Sue Korpan. (Gilbert photo)

Irving Eldredge's English Foxhound Ch. Mr. Stewart's Cheshire Winslow made dog show buffs sit up and take notice when he appeared at shows along the east coast. His great type and perfect attitude set a standard for the breed that stands to this day. This photo was taken by the author before Winslow made his show ring debut.

"The Golden One," Margaret Newcombe's incomparable Whippet import, Ch. Courtenay Fleetfoot of Pennyworth. He was handled by Bob Forsyth to a record seldom achieved by any American show dog—thirty-six times shown, with twenty-one Bests in Show, thirty-two Hound Group Firsts, three Group Placements, and only one defeat in the Breed! Yet what truly lives on as his legacy is his great contribution as a sire of forty-five champions, many of which worked in tandem with American bloodlines to produce the great kennels of succeeding generations. (Ben Burwell photo)

Noted worldwide as the home of some of the finest Clumber Spaniels produced in recent decades, Ch. Clussexx Billy Goat's Gruff stands among the best, developed through the breeding talents of Doug Johnson. Johnson himself says that "this Clumber Spaniel embodies all the proper elements which define type in the breed—lovely head, neck, and topline, massive bone, and depth of body. They all come together with the essential lip, loose skin, proper eye placement and lid shape." (The requisite "Spaniel roundness" Johnson also points out can be better seen in the movement picture of Billy in Chapter 5.) (Wayne Cott photo)

62 Solving the Mysteries of Breed Type

*Few dogs earn the relatively unanimous admiration that Chris Terrell's famous Afghan Hound Ch. Kabik's the Challenger achieved during his show career. His photographs and likeness appear so frequently when ideal type is discussed in this breed that awarding him icon status seems almost inadequate. "Pepsi" is pictured being examined by Derek Rayne at the **Kennel Review** magazine Tournament of Champions, where he went on to become supreme Showdog of the Year. (Booth photo)*

Alva Rosenberg was but one of the many knowledgeable judges who admired the qualities of Julie Gasow's Dick Cooper handled Ch. Salilyn's Aristocrat. "Risto" was a pillar of the Salilyn breeding program and served to establish his type and style for succeeding generations. (Ritter photo)

Chapter 4   Defining the Term   63

Patricia Craige Trotter's Vin-Melca Norwegian Elkhound Kennel produced a wealth of famous champions over the last half century, but none generated more interest in the breed than the popular Ch. Vin Melca's Vagabond. Vagabond was owner-handled to Top Dog All Breeds in 1970. His elegance and charismatic deportment were passed on to succeeding generations and took the Vin-Melca breeding program a great stride forward. (Photo courtesy of Patricia Craige Trotter)

To be considered one of the best of his time, if not of all time, is indeed an achievement for parti-color Cocker Spaniel Ch. Dau Han's Dan Morgan. He earned his reputation in the Golden Age of the breed—when the American Cocker was indeed King of the Sporting Group. His type set the standard for the Variety, and duplicating it became the element of success. (Rudolf Tauskey photo)

64 Solving the Mysteries of Breed Type

Ch. St. Aubrey's Dragonora Of Elsdon conceded nothing to the competition in this normally male-dominated breed. She captured the essence of the breed in type, size, coat, and presentation. Her Best in Show award at Westminster in 1982 was undoubtedly one of the most popular wins taken at that stellar event. She is pictured here winning Best in Show under judge Miss Gladys R. Groskin. She was handled by Bill Trainor for owner Mrs. Anne E. Snelling. (Tatham photo)

The untimely death of Jeff and Nan Eisley Bennett's Ch. TuRo's Futurian Of Cachet came as a shock to the entire Boxer world, limiting the opportunity of many who had wished to take advantage of his outstanding quality in their breeding program. However, the offspring he did produce stand in testimony to his great type. He was handled throughout his career by Gary Steele. (Cook photo)

Fans of Boston Terrier Ch. El-bo's Rudy Is A Dandy often said that Rudy handled his owner to an unusually fine record of wins. Always handled by breeder-owner Bob Candland, Rudy became the Top Winning Dog of All Time in his breed in the early 1980s and maintains that position to this day. Internationally renowned judge Reiner Voorhinen awarded Rudy the Non Sporting Group when he judged at Santa Barbara K.C. and said, "By far the best Boston Terrier I have seen anywhere in the world!" (Ludwig photo)

All of us who first laid eyes on Ed Dalton's import Ch. Ttarb The Brat knew he was destined for stardom. What we could not know is that in addition to retiring with sixty all-breed Best in Show wins, he would so profoundly impact the Smooth Fox Terrier breed. His one hundred champion sons and daughters provided an entire renaissance in the the Smooth breed. The Brat was handled throughout his career by Ric Chashoudian and his former wife Sandi Chashoudian. Photo taken by the author at the Brat's first viewing—Santa Barbara, 1979.

66   Solving the Mysteries of Breed Type

Few German Shepherds are able to satisfy both breed specialist and all-around judges. Jane Firestone's Jimmy Moses-handled Ch. Altana's Mystique was a noted exception, winning over two hundred all-breed Bests in Show and countless Specialty wins under some of the breed's most respected breeder-judges. Without a doubt, her beautiful breed type and solid character earn her a place of distinction in the annals of purebred dogs for all time to come. (Warren Cook photo)

Even the rarest of breeds needs a goal to measure progress by, and the excellent Sussex Spaniel Ch. Clussexx Three D Grinchey Glee easily provides that for his breed. Type in the Sussex is long, low, level of back, large of bone, and golden liver in color. This dog is all that and meets the breed's greatest challenge with strength—staying low with enough upper arm to be functional. Grinchey Glee was winner of both the National Specialty and Best of Breed at Westminster Kennel Club in 2001. (Downey phot)

*This incomparable Lhasa Apso, English Champion Saxonspring's Fresno, has been hailed by many breed experts as one of the finest—if not **the** finest—ever bred. Bred by Jean Blythe in England and owned and campaigned to a phenomenal record by Geoff Corish, Fresno retired to a carefree life at the home of her owner, where she lived until she was seventeen and a half years old. (Photo courtesy of Geoff Corish)*

Statistics—love 'em or leave 'em

Some of the dogs that I included were those who had acquired great show records; others earned their respect as producers. Some were little known other than to the aficionados of their respective breeds. As I progressed, it became glaringly apparent that show records were inconsequential in my search; yesterday's yardstick for show-ring success would always pale beside what was needed just a decade later.

Does the fact that dogs win more today mean they are better than those shown in the '50s or '60s? Hardly. There are simply more opportunities to amass numbers—more shows, more highly developed and accessible methods of transporting dogs and exhibitors. If numbers were used to measure quality in a dog, then stamina would have to be included as an element of type. If you do not believe stamina on the part of both handler and dog is important to coming out on top in the statistics, try keeping up with any of the teams in the top few places of their respective groups.

My discussions regarding great dogs past and present also made me very much aware of what an intrinsic part interpretation and opinion play in the dog game—the great latitude it provides its players to create their own version of reality. The structure of the game lends itself to a belief that "as we see it" is as valid as what is actually so. However, the really successful players appear to be those who value their own knowledge and opinion but remain open to any input that would help expand their personal vision. They are those who never stop learning.

Breed standards do allow the reader to interpret. A judge's opinion is based upon what he or she believes to be correct. A dog's loss in the ring is due to what the handler rationalizes the reason is.

Even things as basic as a dog's ability to produce quality or a handler's gifted hands are subject to the viewer's assessment. The reason for this, of course, is that there is no finish line to cross, no end zone in which to score a touchdown, no high jump to clear.

I think this is why statistics measuring a dog's accomplishments in the ring or as a producer have gained such a strong but perhaps overly important foothold in the modern dog game. They seemingly provide a source of authority for opinion—presumably a dog capable of amassing the numbers revealed by the statistics is superior to those that have not. In some cases this is true, and in other cases it is not so true. Numbers tell us nothing of a dog's worth—that is entirely dependent upon our own ability to evaluate the dog or the quality of get produced.

Who's to blame?

Numbers in themselves can't be guilty, innocent, or responsible for anything. They are simply numbers. It's what we do with them that causes the problems. Blaming numbers—the dog press that publishes them and the professional handlers who are paid to acquire them—for the "downfall of the dog game" is nonsense.

The dog publications, some of which also do an excellent job of educating, are our modern-day method of national and international communication. American dog publications, other than perhaps the American Kennel Club's *AKC Gazette*, survive or fail through advertising.

They tally and publish statistics as loss leaders—at their own expense—to encourage and attract life-blood advertising. There is no obligation on the part of anyone to subscribe to the publications, to pay any attention to the published statistics, or to advertise. Doing so depends entirely upon the owners of the dogs.

Professional handlers are employed to do the job that most owners do not have the time, talent, or endurance to do themselves. Their acquiring the mega-records they sometimes do for their clients is the service provided for a fee. No one is required to employ a professional handler or to seek huge show records. Again, a matter of choice.

Blaming publications for problems that exist in the dog game when their use is entirely optional shifts responsibility from its source. I think it is the breeder and judge who might look to themselves regarding how much weight they give over to publications and numbers.

Statistics do not insist a breeder use a dog at stud, nor do they dictate which dog a judge must put up or down. Those are decisions for which the breeder and judge alone are responsible for making.

If an individual wants to really learn to appreciate and understand—better yet, to be able to recognize outstanding type—common sense demands reality not be distorted by numbers, egos, or blame.

Where type prevails

All this takes us back to our collection of dogs that have achieved admiration because of their outstanding type—some of them big winners, some of them not.

One of the first that came to mind was the Irish Terrier icon Ch. Rock Ledge Mac Michael. The first time I ever saw Michael was long before he became world famous—in fact, before he had even embarked on his highly successful show career. The scene was a Southern California puppy match.

I had a break of a few minutes between breeds and looked on into the next ring. Wood Wornell was standing there with a five-month-old puppy that all but took my breath away!

I turned to Fran Cazier, who was my ring steward on the day, and said, "Fran, is that not the most perfect thing you have ever seen in your life?" Little Michael won the Breed that day and proceeded to win the Puppy Group.

I was doing Best in Match, and though Dolly Ward was showing a smashing Samoyed youngster and Joel Marston was there with one of the stunning Starcrest Chow Chows, I could only see young Michael. It was his first Best in Match; his first show, in fact.

I recall just as vividly my introduction to two then-unshown dogs, later to become show-ring greats in the hands of professional handler George Alston. On separate occasions, George gave me a preview of his two "winners-to-be" with no introduction outside of, "I want to show you something." Each dog came out of its crate, stretched, and without being touched struck a pose that epitomized everything I could imagine their breeds might aspire to.

One of the dogs was the unforgettable Irish Setter Ch. McCammon's Marquis. The other was the splendid English Foxhound Ch. Mr. Stewart's Cheshire Winslow.

Marquis was big, big and beautiful. But even those who would have wished him smaller had trouble denying the dog. He was a one-in-a-million kind of a dog. Granted, he had more size than he would have needed, but every additional inch was more exquisite than the inch before. Bone, power, and substance combined with a unique athleticism and striking Irish type. He enjoyed a great show career, but no greater tribute could ever have been paid the dog than that which the Irish Setter Club of America, Inc. gave Marquis. He was used as the model for the Irish Setter Illustrated Standard published by that organization.

In truth, I knew nothing of English Foxhounds when I first laid eyes on "Winslow," but what I saw convinced me I was observing something rare indeed. I had my camera with me that day and took a whole series of pictures. I knew this was a dog that would definitely find a page in dog-show history. That he did.

Reflection brought to mind Peggy Newcombe's "Golden One," the incomparable Whippet, Ch. Courtenay Fleetfoot of Pennyworth. I was present for each of his wins of the three jewels in what we then called the "Triple Crown"—New York's Westminster, Chicago's International, and California's Harbor Cities. This was a dog whose host of admirers included many of Whippetdom's most knowledgeable. A mighty winner, and equally impressive sire.

Julie Gasow's fabulous Ch. Salilyn's Aristocrat had always held my admiration as a show dog, but it wasn't until well after his retirement in 1975 that I had an opportunity to appreciate his incredible beauty as a Springer. There was a once-in-a-lifetime exhibition of "Risto" and another of my all-time favorites, his great winning son, Ch. Chinoe's Adamant James.

Adamant James had won Best in Show twice in succession at Westminster Kennel Club—1971 and 1972. These back-to-back wins were a feat that hadn't been duplicated since the Doberman Ch. Rancho Dobe's Storm had done so in 1952 and 1953.

The exhibition of the two was yet another historic event for me at Detroit Kennel Club, but even more significant was seeing the two great Springers standing side by side and realizing that even among breed icons there is a difference. Risto provided that moment of enlightenment, which has lasted an entire lifetime when I stop to consider Springer type.

There has been a whole legion of dogs that I include in my roster of dogs of great type: Chris Terrell's unforgettable "Pepsi," Ch. Kabik's The Challenger; Pat Craige Trotter's Ch. Vin-Melca's Vagabond; Muriel Laubach's parti-color Cocker, Ch. Dau Han's Dan Morgan; Anne Snelling's Peke bitch, Ch. St. Aubrey Dragonora of Elsdon; Jeff and Nan Eisley Bennett's Boxer, Ch. TuRo's Futurian of Cachet; and Bob Candland's unforgettable Boston Terrier, Ch. El-bo's Rudy Is A Dandy.

Those, of course, are all famous, but there were and are many lesser-known but just as exemplary breed representatives—names that aren't necessarily associated with mega-show records but whose quality warrants their being included. They, along with the more famous, appear in this and other chapters of the book.

The common denominator of all of these dogs was breed type, of course. That is what brought them together, but my purpose in doing this retrospective was to discern what specifically it was that allowed them to be categorized as such.

What I began to realize was that each of these dogs shared certain specific characteristics in which they could be scored very heavily. These high scores were not in just one or two respects but in a number of them. It is the sum of these characteristics that provided the basis—the very essence—of their being included in the elite group they were in. I began to realize that these were the essentials that did in fact define breed type. I also began to see that all representative purebred dogs possess these essentials, but it is the degree to which they excel in them that determines where the dogs will rank on the scale of excellence.

Assignment

Practice makes perfect, and there are a number of opportunities throughout the following chapters to put what you read into practice. Here are a few suggestions that will help you develop your understanding of what type actually is.

1. Develop a list of the dogs in your breed or the breed you are studying that have the reputation of excelling in type.

2. If the breed is new to you, speak to the individuals in the breed who have successfully bred and shown quality dogs over the years. Be sure to explain what you are after so that the person you are requesting the information from does not think you are compiling list of dogs that are simply famous.

3. Ask these experienced individuals to tell you what their specific reasons are for designating the dog or dogs as having outstanding type.

Part II

The Five Elements of Breed Type

5 | The Common Denominators

*S*o, what do the dogs included in our informal "Breed Type Hall of Fame" have in common? What is it that earns dogs this kind of distinction? Even more important, what is it they have that will be of assistance to us as we compare them to other dogs of their respective breeds or to dogs of other breeds?

There could easily be as many opinions of what this rarefied group has in common as we have opinion givers. However, opinion is not what we are looking for here. Popular opinion may tell us type lies entirely in a breed's head or in some other isolated characteristic.

Obviously, it's not something that is transferable—that is, not something that will bring agreement from fanciers of all breeds. A Bulldog or Collie fancier might tells us type lies in the breed's head, but I seriously doubt someone from German Shepherds would support that theory.

The answer to what ties together the individuals selected on the basis of breed type lies beyond what is peculiar to any one breed. The most important clues are found in breed standards and the breed's origin—not in what any one standard says about its own breed, but in what the message is in *all* breed standards.

The question then is, what do all breed standards speak to? The answer, without a doubt, is origin and purpose. It's in that message that we find the characteristics that enable a breed to be what it was intended to be. There was an intention—a purpose—in every breed developed.

Although some may consider the job performed by a herding dog of greater significance than that of a dog of a purely decorative breed, both have *purpose*—one to work in a particular manner, the other to please in a certain way.

The purpose of the Shetland Sheepdog is to herd. The breed's place of origin and the stock it worked dictated economy of size. The characteristics that permitted the breed to fulfill its purpose constitute a governing part of its essence. Noel Bosse's Ch. Banchory Thousands Cheered gives every indication she would be capable of functioning in the capacity for which the breed was intended. She is pictured here winning Best in Show under judge Dr. Alvin Krause. (Petrulis photo).

*Despite the fact that the ancient Maltese does not work the flocks or guard the home, he has no less a purpose in life than its harder-working cousins. Through history, learned authors have sung the praises of this diminutive breed, and Dr. Caius, physician to Queen Elizabeth, captured both the essence and purpose of the breed beautifully in the year 1570 when he wrote, "That kind is very small indeed and chiefly sought after for the pleasure and amusement of women. The smaller the kind, the more pleasing it is." The **purpose** for the breed, then, is to **please**. This reason is perhaps not as vital to human existence as the Shetland Sheepdog's, but we need only to look around ourselves to see how much of what we have and do is for pleasure rather than sustenance. There can be no doubt that Ch. Sand Island Small Kraft Lite, pictured here with Vicki Abbott, is totally suited to fulfill his breed's purpose. (Photo courtesy of Vicki Abbott)*

The purpose of the Shetland Sheepdog is to herd. The purpose of the Maltese is to please with its distinctive beauty points and pleasing personality. The essence of both these breeds lies in their being able to fulfill their purpose.

The dog having a preponderance of the breed characteristics that allow it to be as intended would therefore be the *type* of dog that should be selected for that purpose. It is the best *type* of dog

As time has moved along, service dogs have had less and less opportunity to actually be observed serving in the capacity for which they were created. Thus, having the characteristics that *in theory* best prepare them to function as intended has became increasingly relied upon.

Let's face it, just looking at that perfectly constructed Irish Setter says nothing about how well the dog will work in the field. It is *theory* upon which we establish our breeding programs and *theory* that we use to make our determinations for awards in the show ring.

The importance in all this is to understand that every single breed of domesticated dog has a valid and specific purpose, whether that purpose is to assist or simply to please, and it is from that purpose that we define each breed's type. If you go away with nothing else from this book, I sincerely hope that you take this fact with you.

Origin of beauty points

Very often, referring back to the breed's original purpose will reveal that a characteristic we have labeled as a point of beauty was originally designated to enhance performance. Through time, achieving this quality in a breeding program or in an individual dog has become an element of success, a source of pride, and, in the end, a point of beauty and distinction. Dogs lacking these important characteristics, then, may well be sound of limb but unsuited for the particular purpose of the breed and therefore lacking in type as we will define it here.

Further on, as we examine each of the elements that actually comprise breed type, you will see how in some breeds the characteristics we assume are desirable from a purely aesthetic point of view actually have their foundation in utility. Consider color— we appreciate how it enhances the look of a breed, but taken back to its origin, the cast could easily have been developed to camouflage, making it less visible to the prey it was stalking. In another breed, color and markings helped make the dog more visible at night.

The latter is particularly the case in many of Great Britain's herding breeds. Their flashings—white collar, white feet, and white tail tip—made the dogs much easier to see while they worked cattle and sheep through the early dark of the winter months.

Knowing what was originally intended for our breeds is critical for the breeder and judge of purebred dogs in that it helps us to stay on purpose. If we pay respect to nothing else, certainly it should be to what the creators of the breed intended. These are the characteristics that do in fact *define* a breed.

Often, what we consider "points of beauty" have their origin in utility. The beautiful range of colors called for in the hues of the Chesapeake Bay Retriever's coat give us a sense of nature and the autumn hunting season at its best. However, the purpose of those colors is camouflage. As the breed works in the marshes and grasslands the colors of the breed's coat serve to blend with the surroundings. Ch. Ozark Mt. Daredevil's earth tones serve as a perfect example of what is being described. (Dogphoto.Com photo)

The eye-appealing markings on a good many of the British herding breeds certainly do add zest to the picture, and when well placed they can optically enhance conformation. Aesthetics were probably the last thing on the minds of the stockmen who developed these breeds. The dark of night arrived early and stayed long during the lengthy winters in the British Isles. Flashy white markings on the stock dogs helped the shepherds keep track of their dogs while they worked. Utility then; aesthetics now. There is no doubt the attractive markings enhance the look of Border Collie Ch. Kennoway Bill Bailey, pictured here going Reserve Best in Show at the Bicentennial Dog Show in Sydney, Australia. (Trafford photo)

How much is "too much?"

At the same time, this knowledge helps us avoid the all-too-frequent mistake of "overdoing." Dog breeders, and particularly American dog breeders, seem in constant danger of believing that if a characteristic is called for at all, then the more of it a dog has, the better. Americans seem somehow compelled to do things "larger than life." Perhaps this results from our growing up in a land of plenty—where there's always more available of something we might like, and the more the merrier. However, there are those times that life, just as it comes, is perfectly fine.

This "more is more" attitude may work in some instances, but let me assure you, in dog breeding this is not the case. When a breed's standard calls for a characteristic, it is usually in a measure proven more than adequate to accomplish a specific end—an end based on the breed's needs.

For instance, it doesn't follow that the Poodle standard's calling for a long neck allows us to interpret that statement to the extent that the breed ends up totally out of proportion and looking like first cousin to the giraffe. Sufficient neck is called for in respect to the breed's history as a retriever. Nothing in the Poodle's origin or purpose required it to reach to the tops of trees to get its job done.

Exaggerations of this nature don't make the dog a better specimen of its breed, only an overdone one. Actually, the dog becomes a caricature of its breed.

A dog that goes to the ultimate extreme in a characteristic so that it is the characteristic we see rather than the dog itself reminds me of the famous Cheshire Cat in *Alice in Wonderland*. In the story, the cat disappears, leaving only its grin behind. Alice herself says, "I've seen cats without a grin but never a grin without a cat—it's puzzling!"

Dogs without type are at the very least a disappointment, but type without a dog is far worse than a disappointment—it mocks the intent of the creators and is what the public, even the dog-loving public, loathes about what some of us do as breeders, even while professing our undying devotion to the breed.

Allow me to give you an example—an incident that took place at the old Beverly Hills Kennel Club show. Beverly Hills was held at the Santa Monica Civic Auditorium and staged with all the associated glamour and prestige afforded those shows of years gone by.

In addition to the many notables of the dog game the show attracted, a good many film stars and personalities of the budding television industry always attended. In those days, I was there covering the show as a journalist and not attached to any of the dogs or any exhibitors. It somehow became my duty to sit with and answer questions that any of the attending celebrities might have.

The Toy Group was being judged on one such occasion, and a leading handler of the day was showing one of the many top Pekingese he had developed a reputation for winning with. The Peke he was showing that day, however, made the non-doggy spectators sitting around me react much differently than the dog-showing set would do.

The Peke was dragging breech coat behind him that was as long if not longer than the dog itself! The dog actually struggled to pull along his huge train, and as those who have dealt with Pekes at all would tell you, Pekes aren't a breed that struggle against anything just to please their owner—not by a long shot!

The Peke sat more than it walked, and the people sitting around me were aghast!

Yes, coat is a good part of Pekingese type, but here an element of type had been taken to such an extreme it interfered with the dog's ability to function in any capacity. Striving for type had created a caricature of correct type.

No breed should have to endure that. This applies to deformities of any kind, physical or cosmetic, that we intentionally breed into or exaggerate in our breeds.

Although I've digressed a bit on this point, it is an important one that those of us who breed or judge must consider. A dog without type is a disappointment, but type that contradicts what the breed was intended to be mocks the breed's own standard and the intent of those who originated the breed.

A dog having type is not the final element of success. The dog must have the characteristics called for in appropriate amounts and in balance with each and every other part of its anatomy.

Finding common ground

Determining this, of course, takes time and study; but without some consistent basis for evaluation of breed type, a student can sit and study a breed until hell freezes over and in the end will know little more than before. Even the most knowledgeable person in a breed will not be of any great assistance to the student unless there can be some mutual agreement as to what the components of breed type in the breed at hand really are. I like to refer to the two being "on the same page."

Chapter 4 dealt at considerable length with the facts that support why I believe there is one, and only one, correct type—that described in the breed standard. Of course, there are variations that fall to the right and to the left of ideal type, but as Susan Lennard so beautifully pointed out in Chapter 4, these are styles—interpretations, if you will—not different types.

Judges and breeders may find it necessary to acknowledge these variations, but it's important that this acknowledgment doesn't cloud the issue. See this as making concessions rather than as granting approval. It is not a case of "anything goes" or, "Oh well, all the rest look like this, anyway." We have to keep our eye on the bull's eye—not the outer edges of the target. They are not the same thing.

Having an "eye"

Through the years, the innate ability to assess breed type has become known as "having an eye." It's a sense of stockmanship—the ability to recognize a fine animal. But yet, even beyond that, it's a highly developed sense of proportion, symmetry, and balance.

Many consider this a gift, and quite frankly I do believe this is so. All good artists have this gift, as do many people whose only association with art is pure enjoyment.

Even with this gift, this eye, it still takes time to unfathom all the subtleties of breed type. Good teachers can provide the proper clues that enable students to find their way to correct type, but it is entirely up to the students to take that information and create an accurate picture. The reason, quite simply, is that evaluating dogs is an art, and like any artistic endeavor, it takes time, trial, and error to hone one's expertise.

You can't for a minute believe that Gauguin or Picasso, Pavarotti or Nuryev began as masters of their respective art or as proficient in their fledging years as they became later. Years of practice and refinement were invested before the world hailed any of these greats for the brilliance they possessed.

So it is with the fine arts of breeding and judging dogs. Many are called, but not all are chosen. And even those chosen have to be prepared to spend the time and study the endeavor will require if they want to develop their gift to its fullest.

And the others—those not blessed with an abundance of the artistic ability required to achieve the pinnacle of breeding or judging prowess? Are these people doomed to failure in the avocation they've chosen? Not so, particularly not if they are willing to study, observe, and listen.

Unfortunately, in the dog game, *everyone* is a genius, and you're as apt to hear someone say, "I don't know" as you are to win the lottery—*twice!*

Nowhere, but *nowhere,* is there such a reluctance to admit to lack of genius as I find in the dog game! I know of dancers—professional dancers at that—who are happy to classify themselves as simply competent and have no delusions about being called upon to choreograph the next major Broadway blockbuster.

Galleries are filled with the works of artists who are happy with any recognition they get because they know that based on their talent, their work will not find its way into the Louvre or Hermitage—ever. I have many musician friends who earn a more than adequate living with their instruments but who know full well that while they may well be a few cuts above average, they are far from finding their work listed on *Billboard*'s Top Twenty.

But it appears all judges are created equal and judge at the same level—*flawlessly!* Acquiring knowledge is wholly dependent upon understanding there is knowledge to be acquired. Slamming the door on learning is a talent most apt to be relied upon by the incompetent.

Beatrice Godsol and Derek Rayne were two of the most knowledgeable people in the field of dogs that I have ever known. Without a doubt, they were my greatest mentors and were at the same time the most humble people I knew in respect to their knowledge.

Independently of each other, they cautioned me against thinking I had learned all there was to learn about anything in our world of dogs. "If you get to that place you figure you've learned it all, fold up your tent and try something else," Mrs. Godsol once said, "before you embarrass yourself."

Closing the door to learning is a major part of the reason that some make such little progress. As a result, they rely on what the other person is doing or what the dog press tells them will make them a part of the "in crowd" if they do likewise. Instead of becoming "one of the boys," they wind up as one of the herd.

Keeping an open mind is critical in any pursuit in dogs but especially in attempting to understand type. It's not that this book or any other can *teach* someone to recognize type, but an inquiring mind allows you to respect the information that can assist you along the path that gets you there.

Realistically, not everyone who chooses to breed or judge dogs will do so at the same level. Still, anyone who is dedicated and willing to invest the time and study can enjoy some measure of success by learning to recognize what the components of breed type include. They are the bottom-line basics that we all must have if we hope to progress and understand.

They are the same basics the mentor must have clearly in mind when attempting to educate a student. They are the building blocks upon which the structure of the ideal dog is based.

After long and careful consideration and many years of observing dogs of the last several decades, I compiled a set of characteristics with which I evaluate dogs. They are the areas in which the great dogs I've known have scored very heavily. To me, they comprise what I refer to as the "elements of breed type."

All representative purebred dogs have these elements, but it is the degree to which a dog excels in them that determines where it ranks on the scale of breed type excellence. The list tells you what to look for, and the amount of appropriate breed-specific material you include under each of the headings will determine the extent to which you fully understand the type characteristics of the breed you are studying.

No one should ever attempt to breed dogs or to award championship points until he or she is able to recognize the degree to which a given dog succeeds in these areas.

There are only five, but they are the five most important things there are to know about any given breed—they are the elements that constitute breed type:

- Breed character
- Silhouette
- Head/expression
- Movement
- Coat

There is little here that might be considered a startling discovery—no direct words from up above, but I assure you a good deal of the mystery that surrounds breed type can be cleared away by applying these elements in viewing any breed you are attempting to learn or to more fully understand. Learning to recognize the degree to which a given dog succeeds in these areas is something that will serve you for the rest of your life in dogs and regardless of the capacity you choose to operate in.

Other ways in which a student will find the elements of breed type useful is in conversation with a breed mentor or when attending a breed seminar. There's a wealth of information that can be gained from an experienced mentor or from a well-presented seminar—that is, if the mentor or person presenting the seminar is able to express the intended knowledge.

Unfortunately, this is not always the case. Not all knowledgeable individuals have teaching skills. The learning opportunity, therefore, could easily be missed. However, if students arrive prepared, knowing what it is they want—make that *need*— to know, the situation can be wholly positive. Keep the five elements foremost in mind and ask the questions that will give you the information you need for each. If you do so, I assure you that you will not come away empty-handed.

The five elements of breed type

Breed character

Breed character is the sum total of all the mental and physical characteristics that define not only what the breed should look like but how it should conduct itself. Edward Jenner and JoAnn Spering's Standard Poodle Ch. Acadia Command Performance combines the athleticism of the Sporting Dog with the pride and dignity of the aristocrat. (**Kennel Review** *photo*)

Silhouette

A breed's silhouette defines the breed's physicality. It does so by drawing a line around everything required by the breed's standard and serves as a prologue for all that must be understood about the breed's physical appearance. The correct silhouette provides the framework within which the breeder and judge will work.

This stance portrait of Chris and Marguerite Terrel's Afghan Hound Ch. Kabik's The Challenger provides the breed silhouette considered ideal by breed connoisseurs. (Vicky Fox photo)

Head

*The correct head highlights the quality dog. Although the ideal head can be reduced to measurements, it is the unmeasurable **expression** that projects the very essence of what we look for. The correct head and expression provide the final brush stroke in painting the picture of the truly great dog. For a perfect example we need look no further than this striking head study of Betty Anne Stenmark's Dandie Dinmont Ch. Montizard King's Mtn. Kricket. (Puig photo)*

Movement

*Movement as an element of breed type addresses whether or not the movement is actually **correct for the breed**. A dog can only move properly for its breed if it is constructed properly for its breed. The Clumber Spaniel's short legs and long body are what create the "rolling" gait that typifies the breed. Pictured is Doug Johnson's Clumber Spaniel Ch. Clussexx Billy Goat's Gruff. (Chris Halvorson photo)*

Coat

This element of breed type includes texture, quality, color, trim, and amount. It should be noted that amount, though usually given the greatest attention, is but one factor involved in this element. All of these factors come into play when evaluating this aspect of the Silky Terrier's breed type. Pictured is Stephany Monteleone's Silky Terrier, Ch. Fawn Hill Lucknow Sweet N' Sour. (Photo courtesy of Stephany Monteleone)

An overview of the elements

Breed character: Breed character is the sum total of all those mental and physical characteristics that define not only what the breed should look like but how it should conduct itself. A dog possessing great breed character possesses all the clues to its origin and history and assists you in establishing that all-important vision of excellence for the breed.

Silhouette: Absolute clarity on the correct silhouette establishes the framework within which the breeder and judge will work. First the framework, then the general interior, and then the specifics, one step at a time.

Head/ expression: Without its unmistakable face and its particular expression, even the dog whose character and silhouette tells you it is a member of that breed would be a disappointment. Head and expression constitute a major part of what gives us a breed. But take special note—they are a part of what gives us the breed—not all. Do not make the mistake of believing it is all that distinguishes a breed. Breed type extends well beyond a dog's head. A dog with the loveliest head possible and nothing more is simply a dog with a great head—not a great dog.

Movement: Movement as an element of breed type addresses whether or not the movement is actually correct for the breed. A dog can only move properly for its breed if it is constructed properly for its breed. When you change movement, you change construction. Attitude, showmanship, and charisma are entirely another matter—they are a matter of temperament and, in fact, are more appropriately included under breed character.

Coat: This element of breed type includes texture, quality, color, trim, and amount. The emphasis varies somewhat from breed to breed. In most breeds texture, quality, and color are primary defining factors, yet far more attention is given to amount of coat and the manner in which it is presented than anything else.

6 | Breed Character

What describes a legend best? Without a doubt, breed character. If ever there was a Bichon Frise who embodied all that was joyful about the breed, it was Nancy Shapland's legendary Ch. Devon's Puff and Stuff. (Ashbey photo)

If you've been reading the chapters in this book consecutively, by this time you might be wondering if I understand that a good part of what I write is considered highly controversial.

Wonder no more—I most certainly do.

I am very much aware that often my lectures, books, and periodical articles contain subject matter that appears to fly in the face of popular thought. At times what I've written may even appear to contradict what some of our most respected dog experts hold as gospel. Certainly those who are convinced many of our canine problems are solved through application, or at least better understanding, of engineering principles must be sure I'm attempting to turn the dog game back to the Dark Ages.

In my way of thinking, a dog writer's primary responsibility is getting the readership to *think*. Agreement and action, on the other hand, rest entirely on the receiving end. In most cases, it takes considerable time before the writer might see any change occur as a result of what he or she has written. (That is, of course, if there is any change to see.)

It appears most people out there in Dogland, USA, fully respect the rules of kinesiology, biomechanics, and engineering. They appreciate the contributions these fields have made to the world we live in. At the same time they have difficulty in viewing purebred dogs as machines or allowing the law of averages to determine quality. They believe there is a bit more to breeding and judging than that—quite a bit more, in fact.

I'm the first to admit that all those scientific terms I'm not quite sure I understand tell us some very important things. But as dog breeders and dog judges, a good part of what we need to know first about a breed usually comes from an entirely different place.

What that "bit more" that many dog fanciers believe in surrounds breed type and the ability to recognize it—what comes easiest when the viewer has that "eye" we always talk about. I think we all agree this ability is a gift—a gift that is not passed out like some free squirt of the latest essence you get passing through Macy's perfume department.

I wish to assure the reader that what I write is intended to be a reminder—that it is stockmanship and an appreciation for the essence of our individual breeds that form the basis for excellence in dog breeding and dog judging. I speak for those brilliant people in our past who were able to *envision* what could be accomplished. Every highly developed breed and every outstanding dog in those breeds is the result of their work and foresight. If we are to carry on in their tradition, we have to remain faithful to the breeding and judging basics that are the resulting legacy.

I guess you could call a good part of what I write "the old-time religion" of dogs, pure and simple dogma—and I assure you, no pun intended!

Members of this faith, if we can call it that, keep a knowing eye on what was intended and avoid extremes and changes at all cost. Their goal is to develop an ability to recognize the ideal and dedicate all efforts to duplicating this ideal, or even if it is lost, make every effort to re-create it.

Even with that said, I'm sure a good many of my views will still set off alarms: "Some dogs may score very heavily in type—even to the point of having too much"; "the responsibility of the dog fancier, then, is to determine what correct type is and how much of it is correct for the breed"; "the danger we as Americans often face comes about through our penchant for believing that if a characteristic is called for at all, then the more of it a dog has, the better. The dog then becomes 'overdone,' a caricature of the breed."

These are observations that some within the dog fancy simply don't want to hear. At one of my recent lectures I was ready to call in the paramedics for a couple of Pekingese ladies in the front row (ladies who bred Pekingese, that is—not Pekingese who were ladies). By the time I got to the part where I gave my little analogy of Alice In Wonderland and the Cheshire Cat and said that extreme exaggerations of type were a "mockery of the breed," the ladies were shifting in color from bright red to an ominous shade of dark blue.

At another seminar, about halfway along, a Bulldog gentleman made a hasty retreat out the back door, screaming, "There's no such thing as too much type… no such thing… no such thing" at the top of his lungs. He never came back, and from what I've heard from reliable sources, neither he nor any of his Bulldogs has ever been heard from again.

At yet another lecture a gentleman leapt to his feet and challenged, "Mr. Beauchamp, did you or did you not once write that you like to see a dog exaggerated enough to indicate he had enough to give away?"

There's one in every audience, of course, and I hated to burst his "gotcha!" bubble, but I did have to make myself clear.

"I do want the dogs I use for breeding, particularly the males, to look as though they have enough of the quality I'm looking for to give away," I said. "But that doesn't mean I want the quality exaggerated to the point of being grotesque or useless. This is exactly what I mean by going beyond type and becoming a caricature."

There are those among us who believe their breed is purely decorative—having no purpose other than to sit there and look beautiful (or whatever it is they perceive as beautiful). Therefore, "overdone" does not really apply in their case.

I disagree. There is absolutely no rationalization that justifies making any dog a misfit.

Breeding for too much hair (all too often of the wrong texture!) so that the hair truly impairs the dog and becomes impossible for the average owner to maintain, or head exaggerations that result in pinched nostrils that diminish the breathing ability of the brachycephalic breeds, goes beyond what the standards of those breeds ever intended. Such breeding not only mocks the origin and purpose of the breed but also shows a total disregard for the well-being of the animal concerned.

Is there a way around these problems? This is a question best answered by people whose preferred conformation puts the breeds at risk to their health. At the same time, I think anyone who professes to have a love for purebred dogs would want to support sane breeding principles and express concern when fads really put breeds in danger.

These examples are extremes, of course, but excessiveness and exaggeration apply just as well to the less exotic breeds.

Let's take the ancient Saluki, for instance. The Saluki standard calls for a "long, supple and well muscled neck." What is described is a neck of the length that allows the dog to easily reach down and snap up its prey. But when we reinterpret this characteristic on a purely aesthetic basis and exaggerate the neck to extreme measures to accommodate a "look of elegance," we defy function, origin, and tradition. The characteristics called for in most standards are there for a reason. We are not given carte blanche to reinterpret those reasons. Doing so works against a breed's intended character, and this brings us to the first element of breed type.

Breed character

Breed character is the most obvious thing about any dog when it enters a room or the show ring. Breed character is the immediate impression the dog gives at first sight. Stalwart determination personifies the Bulldog. The slender bone and light-footed agility and far-seeing gaze of the Saluki transport us swiftly across the desert sand, while the Bullmastiff assures us we need fear no danger.

Breed character is at once physical and mental. It is all about whether or not the dog carries itself and acts as it should for that specific breed. The questions that must be asked when assessing a breed's character are, "Does the dog convey the *essence* of its breed?"; "does it in fact have the attitude and deportment essential to a dog of that kind?"; "is the dog able to be what is intended?"

Many experienced judges say breed character is one of the most important things they look for in evaluating a dog. To put it in as simple terms as possible, one could define breed character as the sum total of all those mental and physical characteristics that define not only what the breed should look like but how it should act.

Breed character is all-encompassing and applies to all of the other elements of breed type. There are qualities that *"character-ize"* each and every one of our breeds—that serve to separate them not only from dogs of haphazard origins but also from all other purebred breeds.

There are certain things we expect of a Great Dane. Regardless of how tall it might measure or how perfectly it fits the ideal silhouette, without the bearing, strength, and power that tell us that it stands as the "Apollo of dogs," it is *not* a Great Dane. Fragile appearance, fine bone, or a hesitant or wary attitude may characterize some breeds, but they oppose the very essence of the Dane. Without the breed's *majesty,* a dog cannot qualify as a proper specimen of this breed.

Not even matching every detail of the Boxer standard's description of the breed's head would mean anything at all if, in the end, the dog's expression and attitude did not say, "I *am* a Boxer, I own the ground I stand on!" A Boxer is compact, rugged, and owns every inch of ground it stands over.

Can you imagine finding a tail-wagging, tongue-lolling Afghan Hound with the countenance of a Spaniel as an exemplary example of the breed? Can a heavy-boned, cloddy, and dull dog ever qualify as a Papillon?

If we can't look at a dog and instantly recognize, by its general appearance and attitude, that it has the style and bearing appropriate to that breed—then it *is not truly that breed* in spite of what a pedigree and registration certificate might say. The dog lacks one of the most significant characteristics that distinguishes it from all other breeds.

And please, somehow, some way, we must find ourselves a way out of the trap that we have set for our show dogs that makes the hyperactive and extroverted personality that may be suitable for some breeds the ideal by which we measure all breeds.

Even the word "charisma" has been reinvented when applied to show dogs. Charisma, as defined by any dictionary you might refer to, is the unique powerful quality attributed to individuals (in our case—dogs) that arouses and inspires popular support. It has absolutely nothing to do with leaping around the ring as though time out for ex-pen duties was in order.

If a race around the ring and show-your-head-off attitude is one that is called for and suitable for a breed—fine. But we must get back to the common-sense place that tells us each breed has its own demeanor, and adhering to it is what constitutes excellence.

Let's take the threatened character of the Golden Retriever as an example. I use the sterling qualities of the Golden not because the breed suffers any more or less in this respect than any other breed, but because historically the Golden has been one of the true "good old boys" of the Sporting breeds.

Calm and collected, he got on well in the field with the other dogs and worked well for his owner or for another hunter who might have borrowed him for the day. At home he got on beautifully with every member of the family—gentle with the toddlers and the elderly, always ready for a romp with the older children.

As we all know, the Golden has become an extremely popular breed, and unfortunately, the composed sterling character and perfectly acceptable level of showmanship in the ring are being bastardized by some in pursuit of a more aggressive showman—a dog that will have greater success in Group and Best in Show competition.

We can't blame the back-yard breeders and pet shops for this one. People who breed at that level aren't remotely interested in how a dog performs in the show ring—they're interested in just one thing: puppies!

I can just hear some say, "Well, it *is* a dog *show*—how is a little extra showmanship going to hurt a breed?"

It's not. A little of anything is not likely to make major changes, but be ever vigilant of the compulsion we have for "if a little bit is good, a whole lot is better." It applies here, too, I assure you.

Still, what effect does this added degree of showmanship have? As the supporters of the one-attitude-for-all school of thought might say, "How could it hurt?"

How? These "improvements" in the Golden personality create changes that are both mental and physical. Hot-wired-extreme, standing-on-the-nails kind of showmanship requires an entirely different kind of character than what the Golden has gained its international reputation for having.

The new attitude takes greater aggressiveness. It takes having an edge. Result? Rising reports of Goldens attempting to attack each other in the ring; Goldens attempting to bite people.

Does that tail up over the back carriage of the "new" Golden come from incorrect construction or from incorrect attitude? That remains to be determined, but what's the big deal with high carriage?

For those who might not be familiar with them, retrieving breeds use those tails as rudders as they go about their work in water. It shouldn't take a graduate course in navigation to tell you that a tail that sticks straight up in the air or over the back isn't going to be much help when it comes to steering!

Beyond any of that, however, stands the fact that there is no greater fault for a gun dog than lacking a compatible nature. A gun dog must, *above all*, be able to coexist peaceably with its fellow canines and the humans it lives and comes in contact with.

This is not because we happen to like it that way, but because this dog is a hunter and hunts in company—in the company of humans and in the company of other dogs. This ability constitutes a great part—some say one of the most important parts—

of a sporting dog's essence and is a hallmark of the Golden Retriever's character.

At the opposite end of the spectrum, the Bulldog standard clearly states under General Appearance: "the demeanor should be pacific and dignified." Under Temperament: "*equable* and kind, resolute and courageous (not vicious or aggressive)." Please note, the italics are mine. Since "equable" is not a commonly used word in today's vernacular, I might add that the *American Heritage Dictionary* defines the word as, "Unvarying; steady. Free from extremes. Not easily disturbed; serene."

I've studied the standard thoroughly, and nowhere do I find anything that requires speed, ground-covering action, or crowd-pleasing antics. Yes, it is a dog *show;* and no, neither the physique of a runner nor an extroverted temperament is grounds for rewarding the Bulldog in the ring. And that applies to Breed, Group, and Best in Show competition.

Allow the Bulldog to have its own breed character and not that of the German Shepherd. Allow, or perhaps that should be *demand,* that our breeds have the character that comes on down through their standard from their origin and purpose. There comes a time when the breeder and the judge must take a stand in defense of character. In doing so, you can help stem the generic landslide so many of our breeds are threatened by in this respect.

*What word in the breed standad describes the Saluki best? If "elegance" is your answer, you fail the test! Nowhere in the breed standard is that word mentioned. What the standard does call for is an animal of "grace and symmetry" but one with the speed, endurance, strength, and mobility to **kill**! If the Saluki you look at doesn't give the impression it can do the job, the dog lacks breed character—an essential element of breed type. George and Sally Bell's Ch. Bel S'mbran Bachrach is ready to do the job! (George Bell photo)*

98 Solving the Mysteries of Breed Type

Everything in the Bullmastiff standard assures us of a dog that will stand its ground and protect at all costs. Stalwart but effectively mobile—the antithesis of what we look for in the lightening rod Sighthounds. Wayne Boyd's Ch. Bandog's Crawdaddy Gumbo's stance and attitude tell us exactly what we need to know about the Bullmastiff in this respect. He is pictured here going Best in Show at the Kennel Club of Philadelphia under judge Mr. Maxwell Riddle. (Ashbey photo)

Chapter 6   Breed Character   99

Does the dog convey the essence of its breed? There must be no other answer but yes to this question if breed type is being assessed. The Great Dane's majesty, dominating presence, strength, and power justify its title, "Apollo of Dogs." Its bearing must tell the tale. Ch. Sheenwater Gamble On Me leaves no doubt as to who he is. He is pictured here going Best in Show under Mrs. Bernard Freeman. He was handled by Carol Grossman for owners Sally Chandler & Chris O'Connell. (Ashbey photo)

The neverending quest for elegance in the American show dog continually threatens the essence of many breeds. The Boxer is no exception. Although the word "elegant" is included in the many descriptive words found in the breed's standard, caution must be exercised in allowing it to override all else. The original German standard of the breed, upon which all other standards are based, called for a gladiator of a dog: "The general appearance of the Boxer is that of a short-haired, strong, compactly built, active elegant dog, of medium height, standing on absolutely straight, sturdy legs, and of perfectly square build." Measurement given at that time for the height at shoulder was "between 17 and 22 inches." Today's AKC standard gives height at 22 1/2 to 25 inches for dogs (21 to 23 1/2 inches for bitches). Today the "perfectly square build" is a highly prized but seldom achieved quality. Pictured is the author awarding Best of Breed to England's All Time Top Winning Boxer, Ch. Tonatron Glory Lass. (Trafford photo)

Chapter 6 Breed Character 101

*The Papillon standard, represented here by Mrs. Elizabeth Anderson's Eng. Ch. Longcrag Archimedes (above), refers only to height with no reference to weight. On the other hand, Toy Group counterpart the Pug (below) gives us no clues in that respect. Breed character prevails with each, and while lightness of being personifies the Papillon, the Pug standard asks for "*multum in parvo*"(a lot of dog in a small space). Neither breed should lean toward the other in character. Doing so would represent the most serious of faults. (Robert A. Hauslohner's Pug, Ch. Dhandy's Favorite Woodchuck, in an Ashbey photo)*

102 Solving the Mysteries of Breed Type

Historically, the Golden Retriever has been one of the true "good old boys" of the Sporting Group—calm, collected, amiable with humans and other canines. Attempts to heighten its temperament for the sake of the show ring are in direct conflict with the breed's character and should not be tolerated by breeder or judge. Typifying the Golden Retriever character is Best in Show winner Ch. Nautilus Saltwater Sugar Buoy, SDHF with owner Rod March, pictured after winning the Golden Retriever Club of Newfoundland specialty show. (Photo courtesy of the Golden Retriever Club of Newfoundland)

Breed standard, history, and tradition combine in such a manner as to make proper breed character something so unique and distinctive for the Poodle that it is best seen to fully understand. It's described as "Poodley" by breed aficionados and presents its greatest challenge, it seems, to males of the Standard Variety—masculinity in tandem with elegance is a delicate balance to achieve. On occasion, nature allows it to happen, as was the case with Ch. Longleat Alimor Raisin' Cane, pictured here with his handler, Richard Bauer. (Photo courtesy of Richard Bauer)

Those who love a breed, even those who have no formal knowledge of it, are often apt to capture the breed's absolute essence best. The epitaph on the monument erected to honor Lord Byron's Newfoundland at Newstead Abbey in England is such an example:

Near this spot are deposited the Remains of one
who possessed Beauty without Vanity, Strength without Insolence,
Courage without Ferocity, and all the Virtues of Man without his
Vices.
This Praise, which would be unmeaning Flattery
if inscribed over human Ashes, is but a just tribute to the Memory of
BOATSWAIN, a DOG
who was born in Newfoundland May 1803
and died at Newstead Nov. 18th, 1808
(Fox & Cook photo of Newfoundland on the beach)

104 *Solving the Mysteries of Breed Type*

The soul of the American Cocker Spaniel is beautifully expressed in this photograph by Wentzle Ruml III. Kind, loving, and happy are characteristics that typify the Spaniel family but particularly so the American cousin. (Wentzel Ruml photo)

Portraying the heart of the Borzoi are the Brothers Kishniga—Desert Song and Dalgarth. The two are considered my many to represent the very essence of the Borzoi breed: masculinity without coarseness, strength without lumber, size with no concession to speed, and endurance. They were bred by Drs. Richard Meen & John Reeve-Newson. (Callea photo)

Chapter 6 Breed Character 105

A dog for all seasons, a dog for all terrain. The German Wirehaired Pointer embodies all the characteristics of the sturdy but agile and enduring hunter. The breed melds the best traits of serviceability and character from its Poodle, Foxhound, and Pointer ancestors. The completely weather- and terrain-resistant coat wraps the dynamic package. Any sign of softness stands in direct conflict with the German Wirehair's character. Pictured is Ch. Hilltop's S. S. Cheese Cake, owned by Patricia W. Laurans. (Photo courtesy of Patricia W. Laurans)

106 Solving the Mysteries of Breed Type

Breed character is as important and as diverse in the rare breeds as it is in the most popular. The newly recognized Toy Fox Terrier (above) is the all-around pint-sized family dog—ratter, vigilant alarm system, and companion. It looks and is quick and agile. On the other hand, the Karelian Bear Dog (facing page) was developed in the northern European countries to take on bear or—if the call arises—any other animal it's sent to dispatch. It's got the strength, tenacity, and lightening speed to do the job, and the job is one it likes to do alone. It's among the loners of the canine world and will toe up to any dog who might infringe on its space. The Toy Fox Terrier pictured is UKC Ch. Golden Hills I Love You Ashley. (Sally Richerson photo)

Chapter 6 Breed Character 107

Finnish MVA and Canadian Ch. Tsar Shadow's The Berserker is owned by Dawne Deeley. (Lori B. photo)

Assignment

Time to do some research on the new breed you are preparing to take on. Even if you aren't looking into a new breed, let's see if we can find out a few things about your current breed that you might not have known or have forgotten. See what you can find out about the origin and purpose of that breed by finding answers to the following questions.

1. What did the founders of the breed want to do with those early dogs?
2. What may have inspired the breed's founders to perpetuate the breed?
3. What other breeds were used in this breed's formation?
    a) To what purpose was the blood of these other breeds incorporated?

    b) What were the undesirable characteristics that these outcrosses brought in (often appearing as "disqualifications" in original or current standards)?
4. Using the current dogs generally accepted as of very good or better quality as models, see how their general character (not specific points of anatomy) would measure up against the goals of the breed's founders.
5. Using the current top winners in the breed for two years, do the same thing that you did in Number 4.

7 | Silhouette

From near or far the silhouette describes the breed for us. This critical element of breed type draws a line around everything we need to know about the dog's and the breed's physicality. International Ch. Ophaal Of Crown Crest strides the beach with owner Kay Finch in this 1955 photo. (Photograph a gift of Kay Finch to the author.)

Respecting the intent of our breeds' creators doesn't mean that breeds can't be improved upon. Not all transitions are to a breed's detriment. Many breeds have enjoyed supporters who have respected the purpose and intent of what was entrusted to them and have carried on in that tradition while making the breed even better. What has to be watched here is knowing the difference between developing or improving a breed and changing it.

The best breeds, in my opinion, are those in which a "good one" is a good one *everywhere*. Regardless of what part of the world in which a top-class dog is bred or whelped, it is seen in the same light by those who really know the breed and is used well in breeding programs.

A top-level Pembroke Welsh Corgi, Pekingese, or Wire Fox Terrier carries its quality with it. It doesn't take one kind of dog in one country and a different kind in another to earn appreciation in the eyes of the breed connoisseur. The intent of the breed's doyens has been respected internationally, and although the breeds have made progress through the years, the progress has been at the same pace and on the same level worldwide.

This is not to say that breeders in one country do not lead the way at one time while another country may do so at another—all breeds are cyclical in quality. However, uniformity of type allows one country to help out another in time of need. There is no risk of having to change the entire look of a breed in order to find one's way out of problem areas or to rejuvenate one's line.

There is a clear and distinct difference between development and change. Development in a breed makes it increasingly more difficult to qualify as a superior specimen because more and more breed details have been fixed, and there is no excusing shortcomings in the perfected areas.

To illustrate the difference between development and change, I've often used the analogy of a man taking a sport coat to the tailor so that it will fit better. He takes the coat there for an adjustment—to make it fit properly. Thus, the coat is improved.

If the gentleman takes his sport coat to the tailor and asks to have it made into a dinner jacket—that's a change. That happening is highly unlikely because common sense dictates the owner of the sport jacket would go out and buy an entirely different coat if that's what he wanted.

We can only be left to wonder why those so intent upon making a breed what it was never intended to be wouldn't go out and buy a different breed if that's what they wanted.

Fortunate indeed is the breed in which a good one is a good one anywhere. A top-class Pembroke Welsh Corgi, Pekingese, or Wire Fox Terrier carries its quality with it—that is, regardless of what part of the world, when a good one in these breeds is bred or whelped, it's held in high regard by all who know the breed well. Uniform goals provide fanciers within breeds like this with unlimited resources for breed progress. Pictured is Tim Mathiesen's Pembroke Welsh Corgi, Ch. Nebriowa Paper Maché. (Photo courtesy of Tim Mathiesen)

Tightening the strings

In dog breeding our responsibility is to modify or improve, not to reinvent. In the early stages of a breed's development, it only makes sense to be more tolerant of undesirable characteristics than we are later on in the breed's progress. We tighten the strings, so to speak, as we move up the ladder toward the ideal.

A perfect example of this can be seen in the development of the Bichon Frise here in America. In the early years of the Bichon Frise's American history, there were many shapes and sizes appearing in the show rings. Champions were made from a variety of "looks." However, continued research on the part of the Bichon Frise Club of America assisted in defining the ideal for the breed. As a result, continually fewer and fewer of the dogs who strayed from the ideal completed their championships.

The earliest Bichons in America were imports or offspring of imports. Novice fanciers here assumed that what came from Europe was ironclad—guaranteed—top drawer. At least the letters from the foreign breeders of these dogs so proclaimed. Top drawer the dogs may have been, but they were in drawers of every size, shape, and coat texture imaginable.

In all fairness, the wide variation in appearance abroad was not entirely surprising, nor was it really a matter of choice. Bichons were forced to survive two World Wars practically on their own in Europe. Twice, fanciers of the breed had to collect what remained—more often then not off the streets—with optimism that what they collected was in fact "*all* Bichon Frise."

The Bichon Frise of that moment in time shared the streets with many dogs, purebred and otherwise, as did the Bichon Frise's close cousins—the Bichon Havanese and the Bichon Bolognaise. It should also be noted that governing European kennel clubs could, in order to assist re-establishment of breeds, accept dogs of unknown parentage into their stud books.

In a 1969 letter written by Albert Baras, president of the Club Belge du Bichon, to the membership of the Bichon Frise Club of America, he said, in part:

> "*We were too busy with our International Exhibitions in Bussel* [sic]. *At this exhibition my wife received first honor price* [sic] *with our Puce (a female new blood). We say new blood when the dog comes from unknown origin… but has been presented and examinated* [sic] *by three different judges? Usually those bichon are really more beautiful* [than those] *coming from usual lines (too much consanguinity—too much inbreeding as you say)!!!*"

The original Bichon imports ran the gamut—tiny, high on leg, long, low, huge, short, straight coat, curly coat, and all the variations and combinations in between. Those who were recipients of this mixed bag of imports were convinced theirs represented the best in all of Europe. There were others of us who wondered whether, in fact, those early imports were the best of what was available or simply represented what European fanciers were inclined to part with at the time.

Breed development

The irreconcilable differences in the early Bichon Frise imports and what they produced made research into the breed's origin, history, and original standard mandatory. The work accomplished by the Bichon Frise Club of America honored the intent of the breed's founders and assisted modern-day breeders in developing consistency in their breeding programs. Their work eventually influenced the Bichon Frise fancy around the world. (Missy photo)

Far-ranging examples of the early years.

The typical Bichon of today. (Missy photo of Ch. Beau Monde Miss Chaminade)

Anyone who has had experience with importing dogs sight unseen from foreign countries knows that the best of what a country has to offer is not always what is exported. Even if "the best available" at a given time is sent, it does not necessarily follow that this represents the breed ideal. There is not, nor was there then, any way of knowing the state of the breed in Europe at the time.

Under these miniature hair mounds with their extreme variation of "looks" were a good number of dogs who showed potential as legitimate representatives of the breed. The problem at that point was finding from this diversity common ground on which to proceed.

The pioneers of any new and/or rare breed have a choice of two paths they can follow in establishing their breed in a new country: either reinvent the breed based upon what is available or research the origin, purpose, and original standard of the breed to ascertain what is correct.

The Bichon Frise Club of America chose the second path, and a carefully considered and experienced committee researched the originating standards of the breed (FCI and French-Belgian) to determine just what the founders of the breed had in mind. As a result, everything in the AKC breed standard finds its basis in the original standard of the breed with one exception. The exception is that the first standards of the breed allowed no clipping or trimming.

Today it is rare to see the long-bodied or short-legged Bichons in the winners circle. Most of the dogs that attain championship status come close to approaching the ideal proportions as defined by the breed standard. Many of the dogs that were acceptable in the early days of the breed would be unable to live up to the level of quality found in the dogs being shown today. The standard is much higher, and it is far more difficult to be included in that special category labeled "outstanding."

Staying on course

On the other hand, a dog may come along in an established breed that captures the eye by merit of its glamour and crowd appeal. As dramatic as this different look might appear, if the dog is out of character for the breed, it is a part of our responsibility as breeders and judges to stand by what we believe to be correct and refuse to reward the change.

I find it interesting that fanciers would abhor the thought of a breeder surreptitiously cross-breeding a line with another breed or falsifying pedigrees, even if this were done to create a greater good. Yet, these same objectors would think nothing at all of breeding to a dog that, for all intents and purposes, defies the actual essence of its breed.

Often this veering off course into an entirely different direction can occur subtly, slowly, with no real intention on the part of breeders to bring about radical change. I don't think it occurs maliciously or from lack of respect for what is correct. Nor do I believe that this might be the first time in history that these drifts have occurred.

I do believe, however, that the opportunities for this taking place are more prevalent today than ever before. Now we have far more people exhibiting dogs simply because they enjoy the competitive aspects of the dog game. They have no intention of breeding dogs. Their priorities might not be the same as what a breeder might have.

"Horses for courses"

"Horses for courses" is an old stockman's term for breeding an animal to suit a purpose. Breeding genius stands behind the creation of many of the breeds we are inclined to take for granted and assume arrived on the scene full blown. Respect and appreciation for the artistry and effort involved should give today's breeder and exhibitor pause before they arbitrarily make changes in the breed of their choice. The breeds drawn upon to create the Bull Terrier are a fine example of British stockmanship and creativity and should remind us of our responsibility to the intent of our breed founders.

The English White Terrier, now extinct, but thought by many to be half of the cornerstone upon which the modern Bull Terrier was based. (From the Kate Sowerby painting owned by the author)

"The other half." The Bull Terrier foundation cross combined the blood of the English White Terrier with the "Olde British Bulldogge." The example used here is based on the more stylized and exaggerated Bulldog breed as we know it today. (From a bronze displayed at a 1983 dog art exhibition in Sydney, Australia)

The body pigment on some white Bull Terriers tells one of the breed's secrets of the past. Although the Dalmatian used in developing today's Bull Terrier was not the modern breed portrayed here, it was none the less an important part of removing many of the Bulldog "undesirables" from the projected goal. (Rudolf Tauskey photo of Dalmatian Ch. Blackpool Crinkle Forest)

Most amazing of the crosses resorted to in developing the modern Bull Terrier is the Borzoi. Here a Russian-bred Borzoi named "Udaf" gives us some idea of how the Bull Terrier came by the Roman finish to its headpiece.

The finished product—the English-bred, South African Ch. Hollyfir's Poacher's Pocket of Piketberg. Owned by Peet and Nonnie Oosthuizen. (The Argus *photo*)

Artist at work

As I've said, I see breeders who were instrumental in the formation of our breeds as artists—their work not unlike that of the masters whose efforts hang in the leading museums of the world. The only difference is that our artists blended colors and shapes on a living canvas that in the end produced the unique and distinctive breeds we have today.

You can't be in dogs very long before you realize we owe the British an enormous debt of gratitude for their uncanny ability to do just this. Years ago I came across a reference in one of my very old dog books that called this talent among British stockmen *"horses for courses."*

Translated into lay terms, this simply means a formula is chosen that will produce a horse best suited to the terrain of the region in which the horse will work. The formula has been successfully applied not only to horses but also to livestock of all kinds and to the many breeds of dogs that find their origins and development in the British Isles.

The diversity of the Bull and Terrier cross

Ashbey photo

Chapter 7 Silhouette 119

The Bull and Terrier cross extended its influences far beyond the inimitable Bull Terrier in several distinctive ways. It is critical to breed type to respect the differences of these resulting breeds: the American Staffordshire Terrier (facing page), the Boston Terrier (above), and the Staffordshire Bull Terrier (below). All trace their heritage back to the same source. (Pictured are: Bonnie Currie's American Staffordshire Terrier, Ch. Fraja EC Winning Ticket (Ashbey photo); Loretta Dunham's Boston Terrier, Ch. Iowana's Fancy Flair (E.H. Frank photo); and Judy Daniel's Staffordshire Bull Terrier, Ch. Guardstock Red Atom (Missy photo).

Hard to believe but well documented is the fact that coursing through the ancestry of today's Bull Terrier are the Bulldog, the now extinct English White Terrier, the Dalmatian, and, amazingly—*the Borzoi!*

Rumors of other widely dissimilar breeds lurking in the Bull Terrier's background emerge often enough to lead us to believe that there is undoubtedly more there than meets the eye. Nevertheless, the end result is the unique and totally distinctive breed we see today.

British expatriates took the blood of the Collie, Bull Terrier, Dalmatian, and Australia's wild dog—the Dingo—and created one of the world's most constitutionally robust and efficient livestock dogs of all time: the Australian Cattle Dog.

Great Britain is not alone, of course. Germany combined Pointer, Bloodhound, and Great Dane types to produce the Weimaraner. America combined blood of the Bulldog and Terrier breeds to produce two entirely dissimilar breeds—the Boston Terrier and the American Staffordshire Terrier.

These combinations weren't just thrown together to see what might result. The carefully calculated formulas of these great breeders produced dogs that looked like what they wanted, behaved the way they wanted, and were able to perform in exactly the way that was wanted. With that in mind, isn't it sheer audacity to ignore the intent of such breeding genius?

All too often we hear things said like, "Oh, I know Corgis are supposed to be short legged and long bodied, but I just like the ones with some leg under them better." Or, "I know the Pointer standard allows a big range of color, but I only like.… (fill color in here)."

Can arbitrarily redesigning any part of what was intended for the sake of another blue ribbon really be justified? Would we condone someone chipping away at Michaelangelo's *David* to modernize the look or painting over a Monet to have its colors suit a room's decor?

This applies no less to the second of the five elements of breed type—silhouette.

Chapter 7 Silhouette 121

Australia's wild dog, the Dingo (above), provided the needed cross British expatriates sought to develop a dog that could handle the Outback's inhospitable terrain and ferocious free-roaming cattle. The end result of a functionally directed breeding scheme is the rugged and fearless Australian Cattle Dog (below). (Cabal photos)

First impressions

As I drive down the street, what catches my eye and makes me look back again is the overall silhouette of a dog. My eye instantly telegraphs the picture to my brain, and that picture tells me that what I see is something specific and identifiable. That is, by the dog's make and shape I see that it is a Peke, a Poodle, a Corgi, or Cocker. Closer examination will reveal how good a specimen of the breed the dog is, but what comes first is the whole.

In artistic terms, a silhouette is an outline filled in with a solid color. This applies here as well. The silhouette reveals all the subtle curves and angles of a breed as the parts flow from one to the next.

That silhouette is the first thing that we see, and it creates that all-important first impression. Every breed has its own correct and distinct silhouette. There is no breed standard that permits dogs to be high on leg and short bodied *or* short legged and long bodied and still be correct.

Those of us who have been around a while have enormous respect for breeding programs in which sires or dams time after time, year after year produce quality dogs that require no catalog inspection to determine their bloodline. A glance in the ring almost invariably tells us.

This is not to say the dogs of those programs are faultless. On the contrary, they may be flawed to a greater or lesser degree, but beyond that they bear a striking similarity to each other. This evenness is due with few exceptions to the sameness of outline—the unique balance of the parts to create a recognizable whole within the confines of the standard.

The skeptic might try and excuse it all away by saying it is similarity of color or markings that lead us to believe this is so. But if this were true, what would explain the identifiable "look" (another word for silhouette) of certain lines in the breeds that are all of exactly the same color or that have no distinguishing markings?

Unfortunately, as important as it is for a breed standard to be specific about these defining proportions, far too many are extremely vague in what is wanted and needed, and others completely omit any reference whatsoever to what is correct, thereby leaving the student to turn to origin, purpose, and tradition.

The AKC standard explicitly considers the origin and the purpose in regard to the Clumber Spaniel's correct proportions. Yet, we find dogs that stand in total contradiction to this important element of breed type but achieve lofty records. The Clumber on the left presents the breed's ideal silhouette. The dog on the right is wrong but all too frequently found in the winners circle. (Art courtesy of Dogs In Canada*)*

Breeders and judges of the Clumber Spaniel are extremely fortunate in that the AKC standard of the breed tells us specifically what we need to know in this respect: "long, low, heavy…he works within gun range…possesses massive bone and is rectangular in shape. Length to height is approximately 11 to 9 measured from the withers to the base of the tail and from the floor to the withers."

Even if we were not given that excellent description, history and tradition of the breed would still tell us a great deal of what we must know. The Clumber was developed to accompany the elderly gentleman hunter afield. A Clumber was meant to be slow working and methodical—massive and powerful, rather than swift, and built to *push through* brush and bramble rather than clear it.

Thus, standard, purpose, and tradition all give us what we need to know. But if this is so, we are again left to wonder how a high-on-leg, short-coupled Clumber can be included among the top winners in the breed, as is all too often the case. Would this not contradict the very essence of the breed?

Being absolutely clear on correct proportions creates the framework within which the breeder will work and the judge will begin an initial evaluation. Once the outer structure is properly erected, the breeder, like a builder, will be able to start tastefully finishing and attending to the interior.

First, the framework, then the general interior, and then the specifics—one step at a time. The breeder should never add what does not fit into the original framework, and the judge should constantly compare the whole and the individual parts in that whole against the standard.

Once you feel confident that you are clear on recognizing the correct make and shape of a breed, you can then look at what it is that makes that correct silhouette come about—the head proportions, the manner in which the neck fits into the shoulders, the nuances of proper topline, and the front to rear balance.

What the silhouette tells us

Every breed has a distinctive silhouette. That silhouette encompasses everything the standard requires of a breed and serves as a prologue for everything that must be understood about the breed's physical appearance. The silhouette not only gives you proportions, it gives you the distinctive and critical topline of the breed in question.

The Brittany standard says, "So leggy is he that his height at the shoulders is the same as the length of his body." The standard goes on to say, the back is "short and straight... [with] [s]light drop from the hips to the root of the tail." (Ch. Sequani's Dana Macduff in a Rudolf Tauskey portrait)

Chapter 7 Silhouette 125

The Dachshund standard requires a dog "[l]ow to the ground, long in body and short of leg...the back lies in the straightest possible line between the withers and the short very slightly arched loin." Tauskey's portrait of Ch. Sheen Von Westphalen gives us just that.

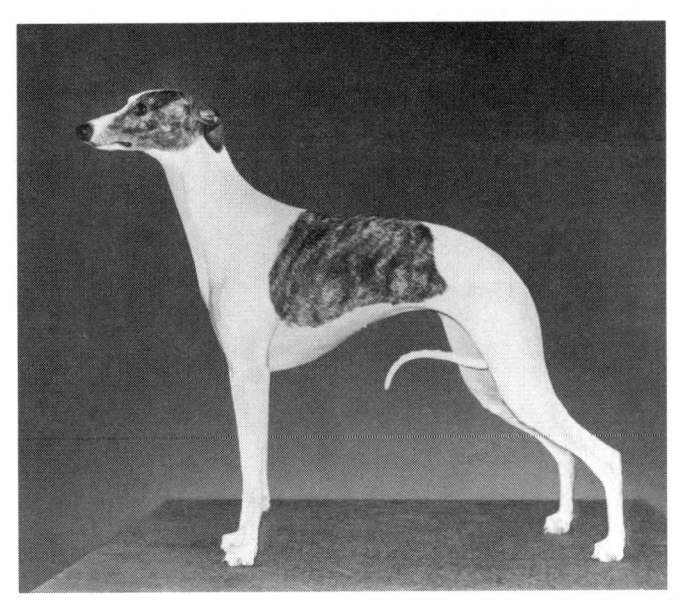

The silhouette of the built-for-speed Whippet has "[l]ength from forechest to buttocks equal to or slightly greater than height at the withers...neck is long, clean and muscular...the backline runs smoothly from the withers with a graceful natural arch, not too accentuated, beginning over the loin and carrying through over the croup; the arch is continuous without flatness...there is a definite tuck-up of the underline."
(Pictured is Ch. Winterfold Bold Bid. (Gilbert photo)

126　*Solving the Mysteries of Breed Type*

According to its standard, the Bull Terrier "back should be straight and strong...slightly arched over the loin...tail should be short, set on low, fine...thick where it joins the body, and should taper to a fine point." The silhouette created by Gordon and Norma Smith's Can. and Am. Ch. Magor Maggie Mae, ROM reveals how closely she conforms to the dictates of the standard. (Photo courtesy of Gordon and Norma Smith)

Line, proportion, and balance—this photograph of Betty-Anne Stenmark's young Ch. King's Mountain Pixie Montizard tells the tale of the correct Dandie Dinmont silhouette. "Length," according to the standard, "from top of shoulders to root of tail is one to two inches less than twice the height." The "moderate in length" neck is "well set into the shoulders...the topline is rather low at the shoulder, having a slight downward curve and a corresponding arch over the loins, with a very slight gradual drop from the top of the loins to the root of the tail. The outline is a continuous flow from the crest of the neck to the tip of tail." (Allen Photography photo)

Chapter 7   Silhouette   127

The photograph of Karen Oxtonby's Am. and Can. Ch. Berlane's Causin' An Uproar, SOM shows us the ideal Boxer silhouette. "The body in profile is of square proportion in that a horizontal line from the front of the forechest to the rear projection of the upper thigh should equal the length of a vertical line dropped from the top of the withers to the ground...Topline smooth, firm and slightly sloping...The back is short, straight and muscular and firmly connects the withers to the hindquarters." The end result is a picture of solid power and athleticism. (Mikron photo)

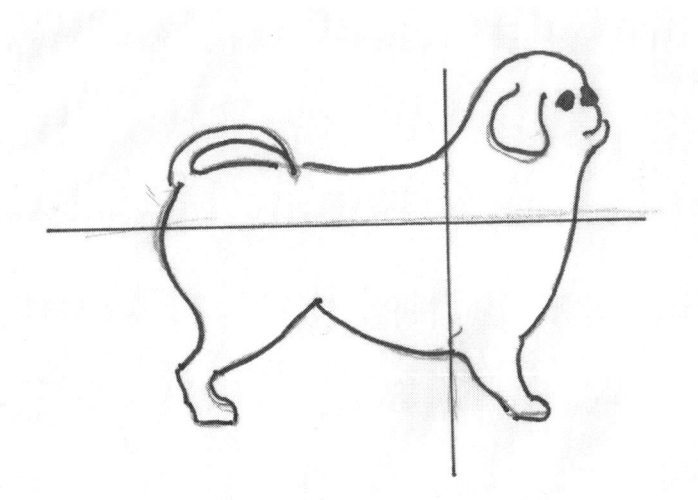

Is a Pekingese simply a head plugged into a mound of hair? Not if you read the breed's standard! It gives careful consideration to line and proportion, like any other well-written standard. Look for a "lion like" image with "a stocky, muscular body...The length of the body, from the front of the breast bone in a straight line to the buttocks, is slightly greater than the height at the withers. Overall balance is of utmost importance." Breed authorities caution against using undue license in this respect—"slightly greater than height at withers" means neither an exaggeratedly long cast nor an extremely short-coupled outline.

What creates the correct silhouette?

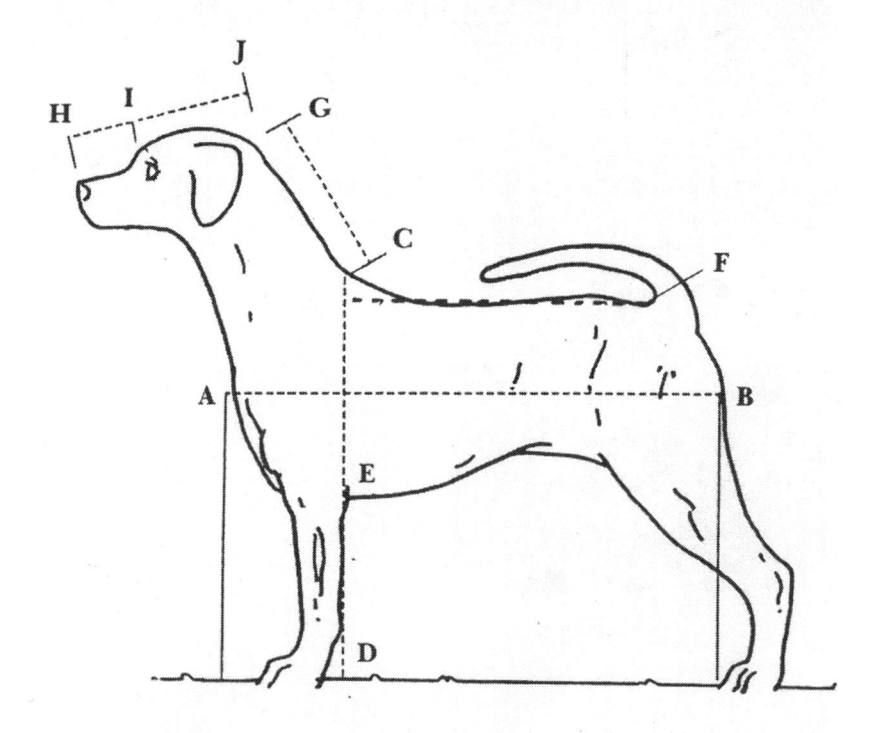

The correct silhouette for any breed is created by a sum of correct proportions. Many standards give this information, some do not. When a standard does not give you what you need, origin and history, experienced and successful breeders, and dogs of great quality will provide the information you need. This illustration diagrams the information you should have about any breed you study: A-B (forechest to buttocks) = length of body. C-D (top of shoulder to ground) = height. C-E (top of shoulder to bottom of chest) = depth of body. E-D (elbow to ground) = length of leg. C-F (top of shoulder to set on of tail) = length of back. C-G (top of shoulder to occiput) = length of neck. H-J (tip of muzzle to occiput) = length of head. H-I (tip of muzzle to stop) = length of muzzle. I-J (stop to occiput) = length of skull.

A case in point

Betty Davey, a highly respected breeder and exhibitor of Bulldogs, knew what the ideal silhouette of her breed looked like. "Bulldoggers," as fanciers of that breed call themselves, have pretty much universal agreement upon what constitutes that shape in their breed. It's remained the same since for at least one hundred years.

In response to the criticism that many people outside the breed made in respect to the lack of consistency in Bulldogs, Davey began to do some research. If there was such unanimous agreement on the proper silhouette for her breed, she wondered, why such inconsistency? Her research took place over a number of years and was based upon the generally accepted "great" dogs of the breed spanning an entire century.

In June 2000 she published the results of her research in the Bulldog Club of America's excellent publication, *The Bulldogger*. Davey found there were certain specific proportions that produced the ideal Bulldog silhouette, and the great dogs of the breed, past and present, matched those proportions with barely an exception.

Davey's research had revealed that there were "five equal parts" (proportions, if you will) that, if achieved, would produce the ideally balanced Bulldog silhouette. They are:

1. Length of head from tip of lower jaw to tip of occiput equals
2. Length of neck from tip of occiput to the withers equals
3. Height from elbow to withers equals
4. Length of leg from elbow to ground equals
5. Back from withers to end of the loins

Davey stated, "The pages of our national publication are filled with photos showing Bulldogs with comparatively extreme proportions...hence extreme variation of type. Many of them hold the title 'Champion.' Sometimes we wonder 'Why?'

"The answer lies in the word BALANCE. And, that is not only the proportion of each part to another, but all parts to the whole."

With the permission of Betty Davey and *The Bulldogger*, I have reproduced the silhouette of the ideal Bulldog with the five points indicated. Brilliant research on the part of Davey, of a kind applicable to all breeds and meriting the attention of all breeders and judges.

Successful breeders and judges have learned to think of this correct framework as the fixed template that was discussed in Chapter 2. They use this template to view every dog and bitch that might be considered as a breeding candidate or competitor in a ring lineup.

The Davey "five equal parts" Bulldog silhouette

Betty Davey, longtime Bulldog breeder-exhibitor, researched the proportions that epitomized the ideal Bulldogs of both past and present. She found that over a one hundred-year period, there were five proportions that remained amazingly consistent on the outstanding dogs of the breed. They are indicated in the accompanying illustration presented here through the courtesy of Davey and the Bulldog Club of America's official publication, The Bulldogger. *The five points are indicated by dots on the illustration: (1) tip of lower jaw to occiput (2) length of neck from occiput to withers (3) distance from withers to elbow (4) length of leg from elbow to ground (5) length of back from withers to end of the loins.*

Do the outstanding dogs of your breed share consistent proportions? Should they?

Invariably this correct outline indicates a good deal of correctness in the parts. As Davey's search has revealed, in order for the silhouette to be accurate, the parts that created it must themselves be pretty close to correct: the height to length balance must be there, muzzle to skull proportions must be in the right balance, the neck must be of the proper length and set into the shoulders of correct angle in order to give us the length of back that is needed. The topline is correct for the kind of dog it is, and the tail is set and carried properly.

In most cases, the dog that appears to be correct standing on its own will also be pretty close to correct when it is moving about. If that silhouette is held in movement, the parts are not only there but also working correctly.

Ambiguous terms

Unfortunately, those standards that express ideal proportions can be remiss in clearly stating how and where those proportions are determined. Only recently I attended a breed seminar at which the presenters spent the best part of a morning arguing among themselves not only *if* their breed was square, but also if it was in fact intended to be square *where* that squareness might be determined. (It was one of those seminars you come away from feeling you know less than you knew when you arrived!)

In any breed we must know if the body length in discussion is determined by a withers to tail or breastbone to buttocks measurement—a big difference. Many standards ask for body length that squares with height but never define where that "body length" is assessed—some breeders assuming it is withers to tail, others claiming it is forechest to buttocks.

The confusion is further compounded by words like *"slightly longer"* and "moderate." These vague and confusing descriptions take us absolutely nowhere and leave us entirely on our own to determine some very critical points.

Another reference that creates unnecessary confusion is the old term "long and low." (In my early years, I thought it was one word—"longenlow.") Long (in body) and low (on leg) are two entirely different things and not to be confused by either judge or breeder. In some breeds, being a bit long in body for what is ideal may not be as serious a fault as being too short on leg. In other breeds, just the reverse may be true.

There are terms and expressions so arbitrarily applied in dogs that breeders and judges may seem at times to be working at cross purposes when, in reality, they are attempting to reach the same goal. Unfortunately, their attempts to do so may be by vastly different, sometimes conflicting, means. It's as if all are members of the same choir, and all have agreed to sing their best but at concert time are singing different songs. Each singing well, of course, but—well, imagine the result. Who in blazes could possibly figure out what song is being sung?

Chaos and confusion is not an ideal state in any endeavor, but in dog breeding the results are found in the whelping box and in the show ring. The longer a judge and breeder remain in that state, the more apt the resulting faults are to be permanently fixed in a breed.

It's hard enough and costly enough to eliminate persistent faults in our breeding programs, but if we consistently attempt to do so by fixing the part or parts that might be said "aren't broken," at the expense of the ones that are, our chances of success are obviously slim at best.

For example, I recently spoke to a breeder whose dogs are held in high regard. In the course of our conversation I mentioned that I was noticing an ever-growing drift in his breed toward dogs that are much too short on leg. The fault, I said, was not restricted to any one line but apt to be found in many lines and in many different parts of the country.

Since the breed in discussion was one whose athleticism could only be compromised by such a fault, I consider it to be a serious one. I had noted the fault even in some of the dogs bred and owned by the gentleman that I was speaking to.

His response was one of concern and not in the least defensive but also one that might be used as an example of how easily we can fall into the terminology trap.

"I appreciate your calling this to my attention," he replied, "and I can't say you're entirely wrong. I doubt I'll have any trouble eliminating the problem in my own line, though. I have plenty of short-backed dogs that can take care of it."

"But the problem isn't length of back or length of body, which, by the way, are two entirely different things," I said. "It's short legs."

"Well, that's basically the same thing, though, right? Long and low?"

"Wrong," I told him, and went on to a rather lengthy dissertation on why that is so. What follows is what I did my best to shed some light on.

"Long and low" is a conundrum of canine terminology that is as damaging as it is persistent. Correctly stated, long is one thing; low is another. Clarity in this respect, as is the case in all dog terminology, is what allows us to make the right decisions as breeders and judges.

So that we do in fact all start off on the same page, let's set some guidelines. We'll clearly identify the three areas of a dog's anatomy involved and list some common expressions used in relation to the term "long and low."

Anatomy involved

Height The vertical measurement from the withers to the ground.

Length (of body) The horizontal measurement from either forechest or point of shoulder to buttocks. (The measurement *forechest* to buttocks can be greater than the distance from *point of shoulder* to buttocks.) Unfortunately, not all standards indicate which measurement is correct in determining length. In this instance, what we're talking about is the distance from the farthest projecting front end of the dog to the farthest projecting rear end of the dog.

Length of leg The vertical measurement from elbow to ground.

Common expressions

Too low on leg A dog can be of correct overall height and still be "too low on leg." This is a proportionate determination. Despite the fact that the dog's overall height at the withers meets the standard's requirement, the vertical measurement from elbow to ground is proportionately *too short for the comparative measurement withers to elbow.*

Too long in body A dog can be "too long in body" and still have the correct amount of leg dictated by the standard. That is, the withers to elbow and elbow to ground are proportionately correct. The fault lies in the fact that the dog's body—forechest to buttocks—exceeds the proportion the standard states as correct for the dog's total height withers to ground. Excess length of body is an especially debilitating fault when that excess length is in the loin.

Once the actual portions of the body are isolated and identified, it should become much easier to identify where a given fault actually lies. It should also become very clear that breeding to shorten body length when the problem is length of leg does nothing to correct the problem. You now have dogs that may or may not be shorter coupled but also are short on leg.

Determining correct proportions

Some standards clearly state ideal proportions. For instance, the Doberman Pinscher standard under "Size, Proportion, Substance" says, "The height, measured vertically from the ground to the highest point of the withers, equaling the length measured horizontally from the forechest to the rear projection of the upper thigh." Further along, under Forequarters: "Height from elbow to withers approximately equals height from ground to elbow."

Short necks and long backs

Two other faults that are frequently diagnosed improperly are length (or lack thereof) of neck and long backs. All too often we find breeders attempting to "fix" short necks or long backs in their breeding program or judges perceiving dogs as having necks that are too short or backs that are too long, when in truth neither one of those faults is the real problem. Either or both faults can be the result of faulty shoulder angulation. As the shoulder blade is set at a more upright position, the neck is optically foreshortened, and the back's length is increased.

In the case of "long and low" we had two separate and distinct faults that had to be addressed in that manner. Here the neck/back length problem in many cases is the result of the same problem and can be dealt with by correcting one fault—the upright shoulder.

Critical terminology

It should be pretty obvious that making it clear exactly what we are talking about when we address faults in our dogs is important. It is important because this clarity can save us all from making costly breeding mistakes.

I understand the AKC is currently doing developmental research in this area. Standardizing terminology and defining *where* measurements should be taken could assist parent clubs tremendously without compromising their domain over breed type.

Governing kennel clubs could make an enormous contribution to consistency by conclusively defining terminology and where measurements should be taken. This would take nothing away from what is the domain of the parent clubs but would genuinely assist the clubs in properly expressing what is desired.

Dog "A" Ideal Proportions

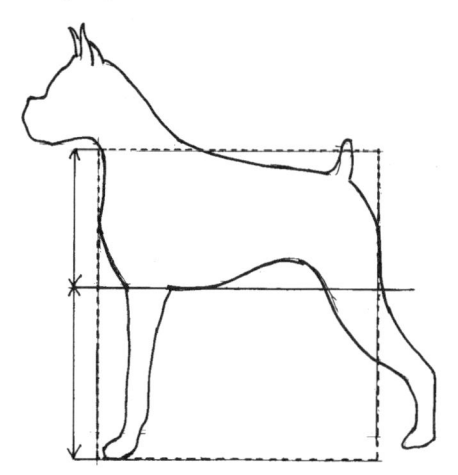

The official Boxer standard calls for a square dog—that is, "a horizontal line from the front of the forechest to the rear projection of the upper thigh should equal the length of a vertical line dropped from the top of the withers to the ground." Educational material produced by the American Boxer Club further indicates that the distance from withers to ground is comprised of 50 percent body (withers to bottom of chest) and 50 percent leg (elbow to ground).

Dog "B" Low on Leg

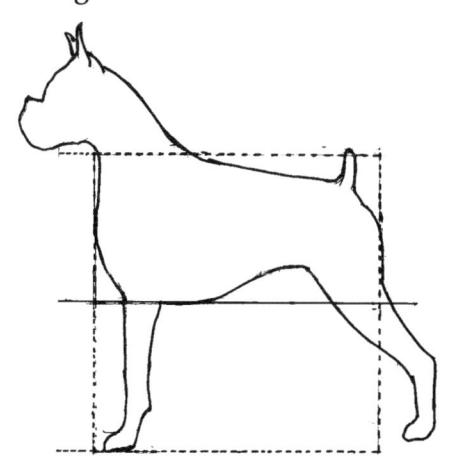

Dog "B" duplicates the proportions of Dog "A" in all respects but one—the distance from elbow to ground does not correspond to the measurement from withers to bottom of chest. It is less than the prescribed 50 percent.

Dog "C" High on Leg

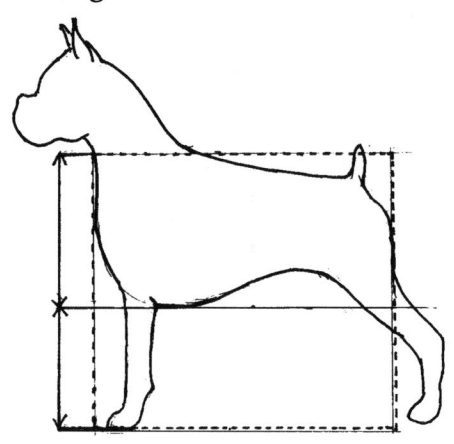

Dog "C" duplicates the proportions of Dog "A" in all but one respect—the distance from elbow to ground exceeds the measurement from withers to bottom of chest. It is far greater than the prescribed 50 percent.

Dog "D" Too Long in Body

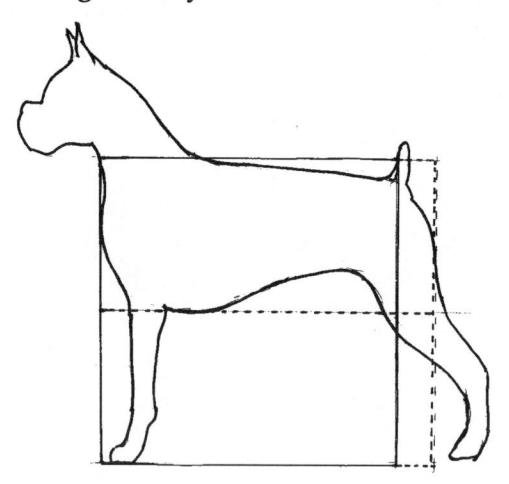

The total height of Dog "D" (withers to ground) is divided equally between body (withers to bottom of chest) and leg (elbow to ground). However, body length (forechest to rear projection of the upper thigh) significantly exceeds the dog's height (withers to ground).

Dog "E" Too Short in Body

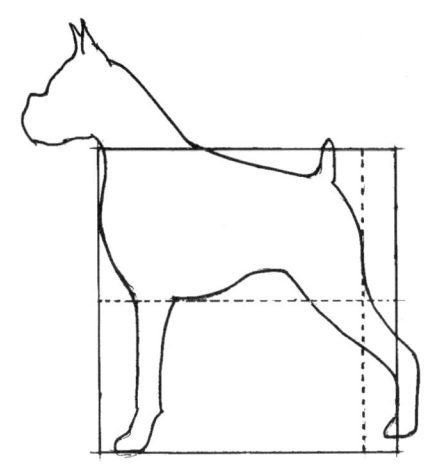

The total height of Dog "E" (withers to ground) is divided equally between body (withers to bottom of chest) and leg (elbow to ground). However, body length (forechest to rear projection of the upper thigh) falls significantly short of the dog's height (withers to ground).

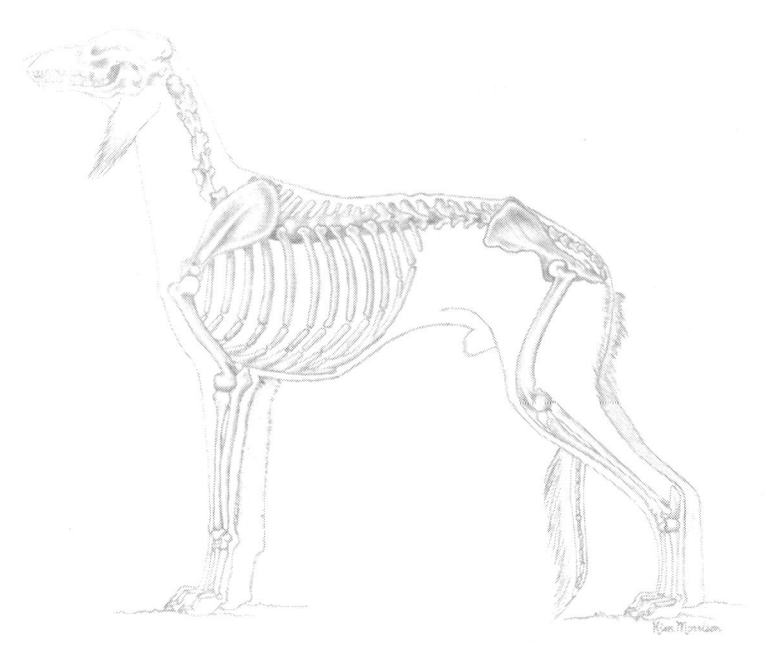

Complete familiarity with the correct silhouette for a breed allows you to understand the where and why of how all the correct parts fit into that picture. This anatomical drawing of the ideal Saluki silhouette illustrates how that silhouette houses all the parts that make this breed operate efficiently and easily. (Kim Morrison art)

Disguises

Hair can hide a multitude of a silhouette's sins or, on the other hand, create faults where there are none. Much of this depends upon the expertise of the groomer. Inexperienced groomers can hide what a good breeding program has put there, and the expert can cover up almost any fault that exists. Thus it is important to check carefully to make sure that what we are looking at is real and not an illusion.

Those who come from smooth-coated breeds may have to rely upon their hands in judging the coated breeds at first until they train themselves to recognize what lies beneath the hair. Scissors can disguise what is really there, but note that I said *disguise* and not change. Scissors do not change the dog, only the hair on the dog. It is up to the observer to see what in fact is really there. A good question to ask is, "is the dog wearing the coat, or is the coat wearing the dog?"

Breeders of coated breeds can be especially susceptible to deluding themselves. Some time back, a friend of mine had a dog of a heavily coated breed that I found hard to like because of the extremely under-angulated rear quarter that threw the dog's entire balance off. The dog was packed off to a very talented handler who was an artist with a pair of scissors. The handler immediately set about carving in a magnificently angulated rear on the dog.

Soon win photos began to arrive, and the owner took no time in letting me know that the dog did indeed have "plenty of angulation, he only needed to grow into it!"

It is the groomer's job to present a dog in the best fashion possible. However, a breeder who reinvents the dog on the basis of what he wants to see is only tilting his breeding program toward failure. Just as much as it rests upon the groomer to present a dog in the best manner possible, so does it weigh equally upon the observer—breeder or judge—to be able to see through what could be a disguise.

Chapter 7 Silhouette 139

An ability to understand the correct silhouette becomes even more important when evaluating the coated breeds. Hair and trimming can disguise or, on the other hand, create faults. The beautifully correct silhouette of Australian Ch. Troymere Believe In Me (above) may be apparent to the practiced eye, but closer examination would enable the person coming from smooth-coated breeds to appreciate the correct silhouette this lovely bitch creates. (Photo courtesy of Troymere Kennels)

There's more hair in more places in dealing with the Bichon Frise (below). Thorough examination would reveal the excellent conformation and ideal proportions of Ch. Chaminade Mr. Beau Monde. It is interesting to note that Mr. Beau Monde, considered by many a pillar of the breed, was whelped in 1969. His proportions were as correct for the breed then as they are now, destroying the misconceived notion that the proportions of the breed have recently changed. (Bill Francis photo)

In summary

Previously, we discussed how breed character expresses the attitude and deportment essential to a dog of its kind. A breed's silhouette defines the breed's physicality. It does so by drawing a line around everything required by that breed's standard and serves as a prologue for all that must be understood about the breed's physical appearance. A clear understanding of these two important elements of breed type takes us a giant stride forward in our attempt to understand what is truly important to a breed.

Assignment

1. In the coming month, pay particularly close attention to the silhouettes created by dogs in your breed that you see most often. Compare them to each other, and refer to the standard to see what that tells you.

2. Form a template in your mind of the breed, and view the next lineup of dogs you see through that template.

3. If nothing specific appears in the standard of the breed regarding proportions, refer to the illustrated standard if one is available. If not, pursue the history and origin of the breed to see how the purpose of the breed might determine the shape of dog that is needed.

4. If you are not accustomed to dealing with long-coated or trimmed breeds, try and locate dogs of that breed that have been clipped down, and create a template based on what you see. If no clipped dogs are available, ask someone of that breed if you can be present when the dog is bathed.

8 Head

There is no characteristic among dog breeds that is more variable than the head, and it therefore imparts individuality to each of the breeds. There is, however, something far beyond what time, tradition, or even a standard can say of a breed's head—it requires the eye of the artist to recognize and really appreciate, for it speaks of the very essence of a breed. Making that exquisitely clear is Mary Merlo's Am. and Can. Ch. Evergreen Chase The Clouds, JH. (Photo courtesy of Mary Merlo)

𝒜t a recent dog show, I had a conversation with a young woman who had attended one of my breed-type seminars. What she brought up was the result of what she had learned during the discussion of the second element of breed type, silhouette, but as you will see it is applicable to head, this next element, as well.

The woman told me how amazed she was at the far-ranging differences in the outlines of the dogs in her breed being advertised in the current dog press. In the past, she said, she had simply skipped by the pictures that "didn't appeal" without giving them a second thought other than "they missed the boat," as she put it.

After having attended my seminar, she began to devote considerable time to tracing the outlines of both what she referred to as her "hits" as well as the "misses." She then started making comparisons to see *where* the outlines of the dogs differed.

What she found was significant. "That line that begins at the nose and follows all the way around until it comes back under the chin tells it all for me," she said. "Doing it that way, where the dogs went off stood out like a sore thumb."

I was pleased that silhouette consciousness was proving helpful, but I did make it a point to caution her about making judgments based on photographs. A firm and fast rule you must make when viewing pictures is that you stay aware of the fact that you are doing just that—*viewing pictures* and not the actual dog. *Never judge a dog by its picture!*

I doubt there are many who have had much more experience than I when it comes to viewing and selecting publicity pictures of dogs. Touching up in the dark room, the good old reliable paintbrush—and now computer imaging—can change the ugliest of ducklings into the prettiest swan in the lake.

Photo "enhancement" is a regularly practiced art nowadays, but it's not exactly something new. Touch-ups have been in practice since Hector was a pup, but back before computer enhancement there was some respect paid to the actual dog.

As early as the 1920s, dog magazines carried beautiful portraits of dogs along with their pedigrees. Dog photographer Rudolf Tauskey was the rage in those days and remained so until the 1960s. It was a significant point in the dog's favor if Tauskey would agree to do a portrait of your dog—you were definitely "in with the in crowd," and the Lord himself knows if there's anything that's going to have appeal to the dog-show set, it's just that. In all fairness, Tauskey had a keen eye for a dog, so he wasn't about to shoot some "two for a dollar kind of dog," as he would say. On top of that, his shooting your dog meant he not only liked the dog but the owner of the dog as well. If you weren't a friend, you could own the dog the standard was written for, and it wouldn't get you to square one.

There is no doubt that Tauskey dog photos remain among the greatest to this day. He really knew dogs, knew how to photograph them, and—if he decided it was apropos—knew how to retouch them. There is no doubt the dogs always appeared at least at their best if not a shade or two beyond that.

What was particularly intriguing, though, is that even with the master's touch that could have made every dog sheer perfection, there was always a defining truth to his photos. Something that was not entirely to his liking might be modified, but there were always those specific qualities of the given dog that were very much *there*—there for the keen eye to catch and appreciate.

How different could portraits of heavily coated black American Cockers be? Tauskey knew where they differed and somehow was able to capture the differences. Those of us who knew the dogs might note the subtle enhancement, but we also knew *exactly* which dog was which. The ultimate value of the Tauskey portrait, then, was to reveal where the dog excelled and preserve those characteristics for posterity. This, rather than to paint a generic picture of perfection.

Retouching is carried to far greater extremes now and resorted to far more commonly than it was, and it seems more apt to be called upon simply to erase faults. Some photographers and owners frown on the practice, insisting that it is deceptive, and make it clear they do not practice retouching—including the word "unretouched" along with any photograph of their dog that they might use for publicity purposes.

The biggest lie

That said, it should be understood that a great deal can also be done to enhance the look of a dog with the camera alone—without resorting to tampering with the photograph. As far as

I'm concerned, the old saw about "the camera never lies" is the biggest lie of them all!

The angle, high or low, at which a dog is shot can shorten legs or make the dog appear to be a canine version of the jolly green giant. Muzzle length can be foreshortened dramatically by having the dog look head on—directly into the camera. Too much length of body can be disguised at a three-quarter angle. The tricks a clever photographer can use go on and on.

These lies of the camera can occur intentionally or purely by accident. Believe me when I say the only thing you can judge by a picture is the picture itself.

This is not to say photographers are deceitful. Their job is to photograph the dog to look its best. I have very valid portrayals of great dogs in my files, and I also have photos that were what I call "happy accidents." These are pictures that, despite the fact they are of somewhat ordinary dogs, somehow serve to depict a breed exactly as it should be.

Over the years I have authored a number of books dealing with specific breeds. In selecting the photographs that would describe breed type, there have been a good many occasions when I have used the same dog to illustrate both the quality and the fault—simply depending upon how the dog appeared in the photograph itself.

This, of course, does not alter the value of developing an eye for the correct silhouette from pictures. Just remember—reserve judgment of the subject dog until you have seen the dog. One of our leading photographers himself said that "if you can't see the dog yourself, a video is the only other acceptable option."

All this applies to "head," our next element of breed type, just as much as it does to a breed's overall silhouette. Photographs of correct heads can help immeasurably, but do remember you are looking at photographs.

It is not possible for the breeder to mate his bitch to a photograph, so when he packs the bitch off to a stud dog, he must be certain that his decision has been made based upon what the male actually is and what he actually has to offer as a sire, not what the camera has indicated is there.

Does the camera lie?

Care has to be exercised in using pictures to learn. Camera angles can both enhance and distort proportions. The head-on photograph (left) of the author's Chinese Shar Pei, Down Homes Black Pearl, portrays her broad, full muzzle. The entire head structure appears relatively short. On the other hand, the three-quarter-angle shot of Pearl (right) reveals the actual length of her muzzle. In this case the length is in keeping with what the standard requires. However, if head requirements were to call for a short muzzle, the three-quarter-angle would not be recommended. Although it is important to use photographs in the learning process, no dog should be judged by any one picture that is published of it. (Missy photos)

How important is a breed's head?

To some, heads are the be all and end all of their breed—"the hallmark of the breed"; to others, the dog's head is simply that which sits at the top of its neck—"a dog doesn't run on its head."

Breeds whose quality is determined on the strength of head alone can be at great risk of exaggeration. Again, one of those *"if-it's-called-for-at-all-the-more-the-better"* situations. Heads can become exaggerated to such an extreme, they not only go far beyond what was intended by the founders of the breed, they become a health risk. It is not *how much* of a characteristic is achieved that is the element of success but *how well* it is achieved.

As much as I dislike referring to any breed of dog simply as a "head breed," when that term is applied, understanding what is being indicated is extremely important. The danger that lies in referring to any breed in this way is that it sends out the signal that head is all that counts in the breed.

Ironically, those breeds are most apt to get by with glaring head faults long before the breeds with more ordinarily seen head types could ever get by with them. Dismissing the intricate detail required in some breeds with "everything you wouldn't want in a regular breed" is not uncommon.

Where to begin

Before you get out the slide rules and compasses to figure out which dog of its breed has the best head, I suggest you first go out and look at some good heads. The best way to learn what a really good head is, quite simply, is to see one. How will you know if what you're looking at is right or not? There is no one who can tell the beginner more than—you guessed it—a good mentor. Left to my own "druthers," I always head for the longtime and successful breeder.

Experience has taught me that the veterans of our breeds have that magical something that somehow enables them to capture the essence of things such as type and expression in just a handful of words. Their chosen words not only define a breed but are such that the words themselves are much more likely to live on in our memories.

Louis Muir's "rapier" comes to mind every time I look at a Borzoi's head, and Mrs. Godsol's "number 10 envelope" description of the head of a Pekingese is just as vivid. Terhune's "noble" Collie head is not something that can be measured but certainly tells you what to look for.

There are those in the breeds mentioned above who might object to descriptions of this kind, telling us that they are far too simplistic. But that is where their essence lies. They help us in creating our preliminary vision of the breed. Is there more detail to these heads? Of course there is, but these descriptions are exactly what give the breeds their distinction.

The knowledgeable people who coined these expressions of head type expected the student to carry their studies beyond the general and on into the particular. I assure any student who sits alongside a qualified mentor through a representative entry, and absorbs what is being said, will soon be able to separate quality from mediocrity.

I try to find breeders who really *know* and ask them to point out the truly great heads in the breed. Please understand here, I am *not* talking about seeking advice from someone who has simply had a lot of winners and touts the current campaigner as "the greatest ever" despite the fact that it looks absolutely nothing like the last big winner or the winner before that.

I'm talking about the folks whose outstanding dogs in the ring have matched their ongoing vision of the breed. Don't expect every successful breeder you talk with to have *exactly* the same vision down to the last eyelash of the breed. However, I think you'll find that, generally speaking, they will have included the same group of dogs in their all-time list or would look similarly upon the entry that passes before you as you sit together.

I have great concern for those breeds in which the truly experienced and knowledgeable individuals have passed on to their reward and have not had their knowledge recorded for succeeding generations. In a good number of cases, it has been many years since the passing of these breed doyens and just as many years since there have been classically outstanding dogs in the breed.

Will there be anyone available to recognize and appreciate the rare great when and if it appears on the scene? Or, as I've seen happen, will the breed's last great hope be "odd man out" and dismissed because it doesn't look like "the rest"?

Hopefully, my reminding those in our breeds who are enlightened enough to know who the individuals are with that important knowledge will not allow it to slip away into oblivion. Those who have direct links to the best our breeds have had must be cherished and their thoughts and opinions recorded.

If you are unable to determine who this mentor person might be, you are being entirely premature in launching yourself as a breeder or judge. The person or persons you seek are out there. It's up to you to educate yourself well enough to find them.

Expression

Although a standard may devote many words to the description of a breed's head, nothing can compensate for seeing "in the flesh" what time and tradition has taught us captures the essence of a breed—the nuances that define the undefinable: "expression."

Correct expressions are one of those things in life *that are* simply *because they are.*

If that statement appears enigmatic, perhaps the following will help.

The example I use in my seminars comes from a Broadway musical comedy of many years ago that has, because of its simplicity, stuck with me through all these years. The play was called *Fiorello!*—named so for one of the former mayors of New York City—and dealt with life in that city at the turn of the last century.

In the play, a little girl and her mother are walking along a street in one of the seedier sections of the city when the little girl tugs on her mother's skirt and says, "Mommy, look at that lady across the street. Isn't she dressed fancy?"

The mother glances across the way and says, "Emily, don't you even *look* at her!"

"But *why*, Mommy?" the little girl asks.

"Because—well, because *she's a prostitute*. That's why!"

"But Mommy, how can you tell she's a prostitute?" little Emily asks with a puzzled look on her face.

"Because she looks like a prostitute, Emily. That's why, and that's enough out of you!"

Emily thinks for a bit and then asks, "But what does a prostitute look like, Mommy?"

Without pausing a moment, the mother snaps back, *"Just like that, Emily. Just like that!"*

And off the stage they go.

The point that little Emily's mother made was that there are some things in life that simply *are*.

Expressions are the defining factor in this important element of breed type, and unfortunately, there is no way to be able to *explain* proper expressions. You either recognize them or you don't. And someday when you are asked by your student why we think they are correct, like little Emily's mother you will be able to respond, "Because they are, because they are."

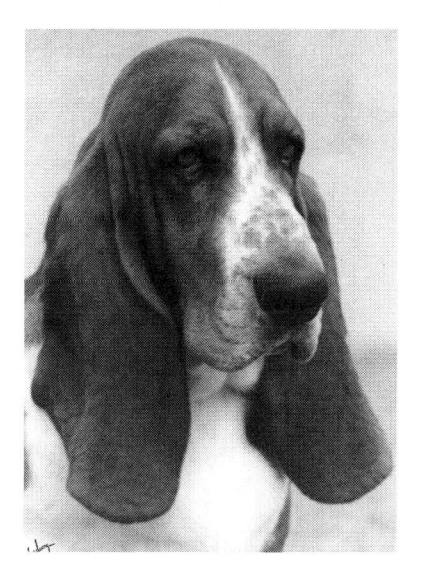

No standard can fully describe or explain "expression," yet it remains a critical element in understanding what breed type is. Basset Hound Ch. Glenhaven Lord Jack (Ludwig photo, left) and Cocker Spaniel Ch. Timothy's Sparkle Plenty (right) have a number of features in common, with their long, low-set ears, rounded skulls, and prominent nostrils. However, their expressions alone set them worlds apart. The one is soulful, soft, and sad; the other is intelligent, alert, and appealing.

The next step

Don't put the cart before the horse. Learn to recognize a good head before you worry about the details that make it so. Initially, you won't know which of the better heads is best, but what comes next will help you with that.

Undoubtedly your mentor will provide clues as you travel along the first steps toward recognition. Were I sitting with you through an American Cocker entry, I would point out the good heads and undoubtedly make reference to the importance of the breed's rounded skull but caution you against extremes in this respect. Your advanced studies would reveal that many Cockers suffer from extremely high and narrow domes or crowns—something never intended for the breed and actually a sign of weakness rather than of type.

Nor would the proper skull be large and coarse appearing. It's the proper balance between refinement and strength that counts, and hitting the mark provides the setting for the forward-looking, soulful eye and the muzzle that is artistic in its nuances but does not lose sight of the fact that this is indeed a Spaniel capable of function.

Breeds in which head characteristics are a strong point in defining breed type are simply breeds that must have great head *detail* before they can qualify as outstanding. Therefore, it becomes contingent upon the observer to know more. Not only is there more detail in the Bulldog standard's description of head than there is in a breed such as the Labrador Retriever's, the detail is far more complex and intricate.

This does not mean that the Labrador's head is any less distinctive than the Bulldog's, only that there is less minute detail required to make it so. An example of the need to understand complex detail requirements will be seen further along in this chapter, where a breeder describes the characteristics that constitute the ideal and distinctive Bull Terrier head.

Head types and typifying expressions

The sizes, shapes, and measurements of canine skulls are enormously varied—more so than any other mammal. There are, however, three basic categories that the skulls of all breeds of dogs fall into. They are determined by the relationship of skull width to length: (1) Dolichocephalic (long and narrow), (2) Mesaticephaic (width and length relatively equal), (3) Brachycephalic (broad skull of short overall length). This is part of the practical aspect of understanding the heads of purebred dogs. The less technical but very telling part is recognizing correct expression. Variations of both appear here.

The Toy Fox Terrier has a balanced head—approximately equal lengths of skull and foreface—slightly rounded skull, and tapered foreface. Expression is elegant, alert, and expressive. (Sally Richerson photo of a Foxfire Kennels-bred UKC champion)

The broad skull and prominent upturned muzzle typify the Brussels Griffon. The breed's expression is described in the standard as "almost human," with very large, black, and forward-looking eyes and a nose placed deeply and between the eyes. (Ashbey photo of Starbeck Silken Starshine)

The head of the Wire Fox Terrier is obviously long and lean, but the standard gives strict limitations to avoid having these qualities taken to excess. The breed standard is written in a manner that precludes the breed becoming a caricature of what was intended. Keen expression is paramount in the Wire, with small, dark eyes full of fire, life, and intelligence. Ch. Dynamic Super Sensation is pictured. (Photo courtesy of Barbara and Frank Swigart)

The correct American Cocker Spaniel head is normal in all respects but prone to faddish exaggerations of skull and muzzle. "A muzzle strong enough to carry a bird, a skull large enough to house a brain," is an old Spaniel adage that applies here as well. The Cocker typifies the Spaniel expression—melting and soft while still intelligent and alert. (Pictured is Ch. Beau Monde War Paint, bred by the author)

Although the English Toy Spaniel is a Spaniel derivative, its correct head follows the design of its cousins the Pug and Brussels Griffon, with the large, round eyes and upswept underjaw. The Standar's design gives us a "plush chubby looking head" with a fittingly soft and appealing expression. (Ch. Dreamridge Dear Charles is pictured, R. B. Fabis photo)

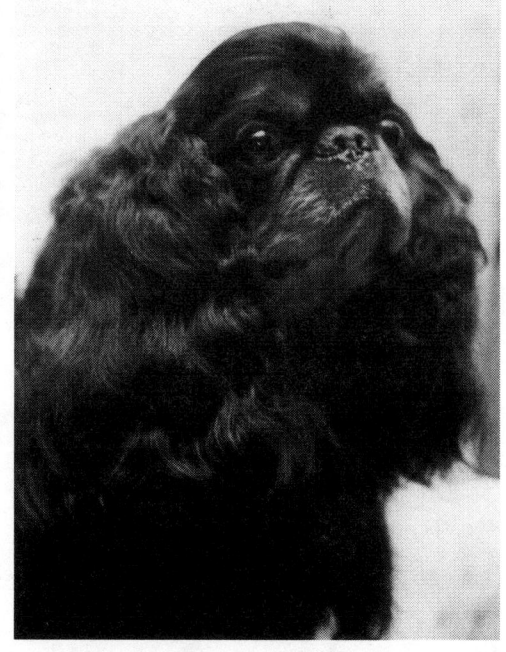

Chapter 8   Head   153

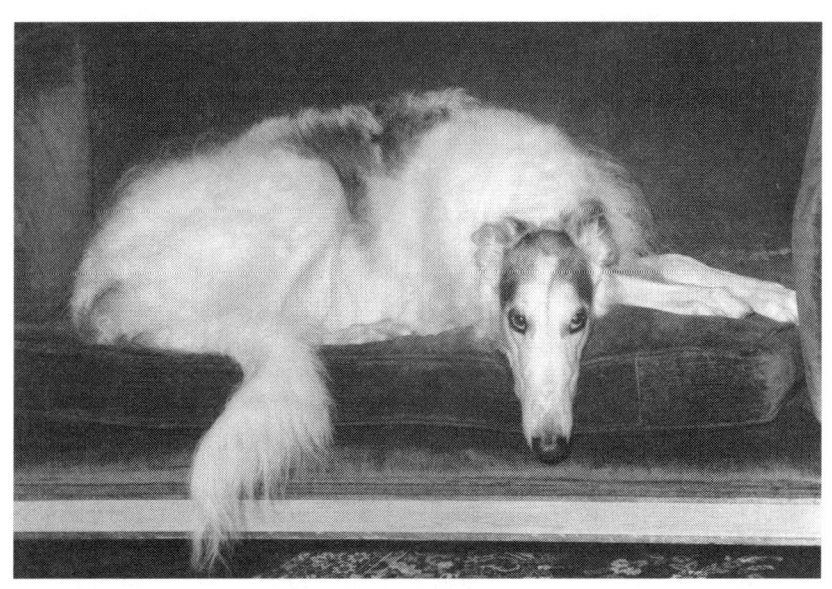

The Borzoi's skull is long and narrow, with barely any perceptible stop. In profile the muzzle is inclined to somewhat of a Roman arch. Like everything else in the breed, the expression, even in repose, is elegant and dignified.

The Bull Terrier head's Roman profile, overall egg shape, and absence of stop disguises the fact that the skull shape falls nearest to the basic Mesaticephalic category. The small, strategically placed eye—correctly placed much closer to the ear than the nose—has a piercing glint, giving the breed a varminty expression all its own. (Pictured is Tamkin Brave Beauty, imported from Australia and owned by the author)

154 *Solving the Mysteries of Breed Type*

The head of the Bichon Frise has no exaggerations. However, black skin exaggerating the size of the eyes, the black points against white, and the head trim create an illusion much different than what might be expected. All these factors add up to the standard's "dark-eyed, inquisitive expression." (Missy photo of Ch. Drewlaine Eau de Love)

Loose skin and heavy bone allow the Clumber Spaniel to plow through thicket and brush. These factors, combined with the breed's massive head and deep-set eyes, give the breed a dignified and pensive expression. (Ch. Clussexx Billy Goat's Gruff is pictured courtesy of Douglas Johnson)

Emphasis

Obsessive emphasis on head alone can be typical of breeds that have regressed to the point where that they find success only among their own kind at specialty shows, unable to hold their own in competition with other breeds of their respective Variety Groups.

The very essence of competing at an all-breed show and having dogs judged by the knowledgeable all-rounder is to keep our breeds honest—true to form, if you will—and not exaggerated in one respect and the expense of all others.

On the other hand, a breed in which the head has been a matter of total disregard flounders in that generic pool from which no individual dog can emerge as entirely correct. In these instances the breed has lost a good part of the subtle defining characteristics that separate the poor from the good, the good from the superior.

Those who breed and judge may differ on how much weight they place on head in determining overall quality, but I doubt there are many who fail to appreciate the dog whose head vividly portrays what we have come to recognize as the breed's ideal. And, in the end, no matter how soundly constructed a dog is or how well its character reflects the breed's ideal, unless its head is commensurate with that quality, it cannot really be elevated to the status of greatness.

Seeing is believing

When I want to mentor someone on a breed, I like to start at ringside, where there will be a significant entry of good dogs. I find it infinitely easier for the student to get under way when I can point to a dog and say, "There, look at this one. Burn that picture into your mind. It is what a head in this breed is supposed to be." You can sit in on every lecture from now until doomsday, read every book ever written on the subject, but until you can really see an example of what it is you're looking for, your education in canine anatomy is incomplete.

This ringside tutoring comes before a lot of discussion on angles, planes, and fulcrums because it is not the measurements that are of consequence, it is what the measurements produce aesthetically and functionally. What I want my student to be able to identify is expression—something that is impossible to describe numerically or in engineering terms.

When the overall shape of the head has been fixed in mind, it's a good idea to see how well the heads of the dogs you see in the ring and in photos fit that shape and where they deviate. Once the dogs who have that overall shape and look have been identified, determine where, within that shape, the ears, eyes, and nose are positioned, and start to notice how deviations can change the desired look.

I'm not saying that everyone I've worked with has been able to do this off the bat, but I like to see how much of an "eye" a student has. Being able to "get it" in the head department without knowing all the reasons beforehand tells me a great deal about what the next step should be in the learning process.

If the student can recognize the good heads inherently, all we'll have to do is spend a little time on the characteristics that help create that ideal picture. Some extra time can be devoted to those things that detract from the ideal head along with the degree of their seriousness. The latter, of course, depends on the breed.

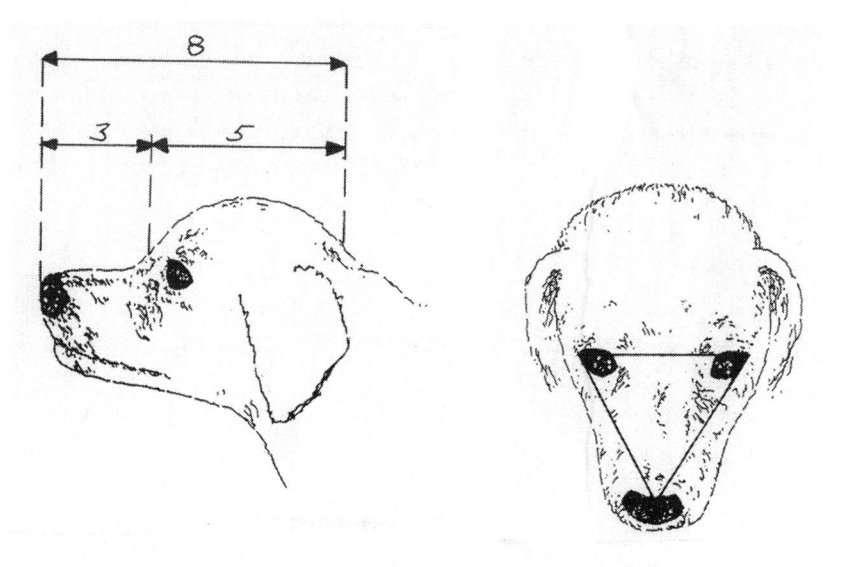

The Illustrated Discussion of the Bichon Frise Standard *gives both profile proportions ("as 3 is to 5") but also the proportions that will provide for sufficient width of skull and eye placement. "A line drawn from the outside corner of the eyes to the nose will create a near equilateral triangle."*

Chapter 8 Head 157

Details inside the overall shape

Once the overall shape and expression become recognizable, you can begin dissecting what has created that unique and identifiable "look." Most parent clubs or knowledgeable breeders within the breed are able to provide the learner with hints on what proportions actually create the breed's face. Pictured here are three examples that help the eye determine accuracy of the proportions.

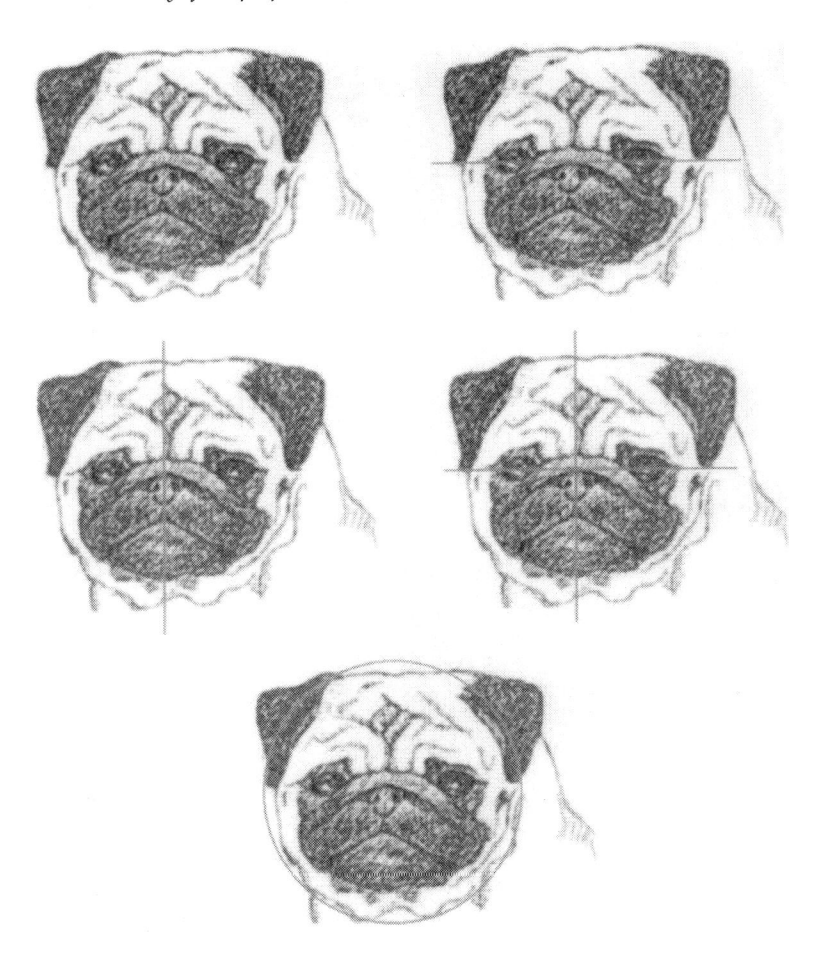

A few straight lines on a circle enclose judge and breed authority Charlotte Patterson's well-executed illustrations of the Pug's head. The lines highlight the characteristics that create the ideal head and expression for the breed: the flat skull and well-placed ear. The horizontal line that travels through the middle of the eyes touches the top of the nose and tip of the alert ear. The vertical line divides the face into four equal parts and points downward to the strong underjaw.

In 1923 breed expert John A Vlasto set about writing The Popular Pekingese *as a handbook for novices. The information in the handbook and the illustrations he had artist Charles J. Allport render for the work established the criteria by which the breed is understood. He was among the first to illustrate the division and balance of the ideal Pekingese head. Basically the system he adopted in doing so was to enclose the face in a rectangle measuring five horizontally and four vertically. The center line on a correctly made head falls directly across the stop dividing the skull from the face itself, much like the accompanying illustration. Because of his innovative approach, the original work has been reprinted many times through the years and is referred to by all who wish to fully understand the Pekingese head.*

Flaws and faults are relative

For instance, marginally improper dentition or a mouth that may be slightly off in some manner is a far more serious flaw in a breed that uses its mouth in the purpose for which the breed was created. It would not weigh as heavily in a breed whose creators had nothing more in mind for the dog to do with its mouth than eat dinner.

"Modern" judging would have us impose the same rules on all breeds—on dentition, on movement, on showmanship. And it is exactly this approach that we can thank for the rise to stardom of the generic show dog.

It is the differences that make our breeds, and there is no area in which dogs differ more than in their heads. In some breeds the differences are so great and so complex that it demands great concentration and longtime study for the average dog person to clearly understand the important intricacies. Breed parent clubs and learned individuals within those clubs go to great lengths to provide diagrams and charts to help understand their breeds' heads and the characteristics that combine to produce that proper look.

Not everyone has that "eye" that enables those having it to put everything into its proper place with little or no coaching. Those who have the inherent ability to do so are not only able to note what detracts, but they also can evaluate how heavily to weigh that flaw. There is no equivalent for that ability. However, understanding the components that constitute the heads of all dogs and their distinct relationships assist us all in staying within the framework of what is correct.

The encompassing shape

It is important to recognize, first, the encompassing overall shape of a breed's head. A square-headed Peke must be immediately discarded. Without the horizontal oblong shape, all head character is lost. The Pug's head fits nicely into a circle, and the Wire Fox Terrier's lean rectangle is critical to success in that breed.

It is the totality of the parts and their placement that create the "whole" of what we look for. This is so aptly captured by an internationally respected Bull Terrier breeder and judge, Mrs. W. E. Mackay-Smith, in a description of the Bull Terrier head. Mrs. Mackay-Smith is better known to the dog world as "Winkie" Mackay-Smith, mistress of the famed Banbury line of Bull Terriers. She writes in detail:

> "The correct head is a virtue comprised of elements which make up the whole. It's difficult to find perfection in every detail, so the heaviest weight is given to the presence of correct shape, fill and turn, giving the head a smooth, powerful and ovoid appearance. Correct details add to the positive virtue of the filled correct turned head, these being a correct bite, correct eye color, shape and placement; correct ear placement and stiffness of the ear itself; and black nose."

Mrs. Mackay Smith goes on to comment on expression:

"The expression is important—the correctly shaped skull is NOT enhanced by large open eyes placed low in the head (looking sheep-like) or large ears set low and pointing to the side (looking donkey-like). The high-placed, small, dark triangular eye and small ears placed close together and pointing upward give the Bull Terrier a very characteristic expression, piercing and alert—this expression is often described as varminty."

The foregoing graphic and verbal descriptions are examples of how vividly true experts are able to capture what constitutes the essence of their breed in respect to head. You should pay particular attention to the fact that as much importance as each detail of the head is given, it is what those details produce that is of consequence in the end.

"The correct head is a virtue comprised of elements which make up the whole"

The quotation, taken from Mrs. W. E. Mackay-Smith's discussion of the Bull Terrier head, applies to every one of our breeds, regardless of its purpose or the Variety Group it belongs to. In describing the head properties of the admittedly unique Bull Terrier head structure, she captures both the distinctly turned profile (page 153) and the importance of the overall ovoid. Azaline White Witch of Piketberg (left) and particularly Piketberg Sensation (right), bred and owned by Nonnie and Peet Oostheizen in South Africa, illustrate the "egg shaped" construction brought about by the well-filled and smooth, clean lines, that are necessary to produce this shape. (Photo courtesy of Nonnie and Peet Oostheizen)

The parts

Within this framework called head and what we as dog fanciers look for called expression, we have the individual characteristics that distinguish one breed from another: eyes, ears, nose, mouth. Each plays an important role in characterizing a breed, but as we move from one breed to the next, we find that one of these may play a larger role than the next.

In Terriers, Collies, and Shetland Sheepdogs, we pay particular attention not only to where the ear is placed but also how it is carried and where exactly the ear is required to fold.

Mouths also play a major role in Terriers, as they do in the Sporting Dogs. The flat-faced breeds demand our attention to the degree of curvature of the underjaw and placement of the nose.

It would be impossible to list here the thousands of nuances that must fall into the proper place to create that "look" that we strive for in each of our breeds, but this is exactly what each of us must devote ourselves to if we hope to breed the proper head for the dog of our dreams—the head that lives up to the concern we invested in achieving perfection in character and silhouette.

Ear placement and carriage

As you progress through the details of the heads that portray the ideal for their breed, you will find that the placement and carriage of the ear often serve a critical point in correct expression. How this is accomplished runs the gamut through the breeds, but knowing where the ears are placed and how they are carried are the clues that lead you to appreciating what is correct in head type.

Bulldog ears—*"The ears should be set high in the head, the front inner edge of each ear joining the outline of the skull at the top back corner of the skull, so as to place them as wide apart, and as high and as far from the eyes as possible . . . small and thin. The shape termed "rose ear" is the most desirable." (Pictured is Mij Charbonneau's "Budkis")*

162 *Solving the Mysteries of Breed Type*

Irish Setter ears —*"Set well back and low, not above level of eye. Leather thin, hanging in a neat fold close to the head, and nearly long enough to reach the nose." Here four generations of Evergreen Kennels Irish Setters illustrate the properly set and carried ear: (left to right) Ch. Smoke N' Mirrors—great-grandson at ten months; Kinvale Can Do—granddaughter at four years; American and Canadian Ch. Evergreen Chase the Clouds, JH—son at six years; Ch. Evergreen Best Kept Secret, CD—the matriarch at thirteen years. (Photo courtesy of Mary Merlo)*

Shetland Sheepdog—*"Ears small and flexible, placed high, carried three-fourths erect, with tips breaking forward." Pictured is Clare & Donna Harden's Ch. Banchory Orange Chiffon (Krook photo)*

Smooth Fox Terrier—"*Ears should be V-shaped and small of moderate thickness, and dropping forward close to the cheek, not hanging by the side of the head like a Foxhound. The topline of the folded ear should be well above the level of the skull. Disqualifications —ears prick, tulip or rose.*" Pictured, Linda Caldwell's very young "Trio Beau Monde," who have not quite grown into their beautifully placed and folded ears.

Cairn Terrier—"*Ears—small, pointed, well carried erectly, set wide apart on the side of the head. Free from long hairs.*" (Pictured is Isabel Eckfeld's Ch. Bellacairn's Bit O'Scotch, Missy photo)

So type-determining are the French Bulldog's ears that "[o]ther than bat ears is a disqualification." The ears are broad at the base, elongated, with round top, set high on the head but not too close together, and carried erect with the orifice to the front. Illustrating the critical ear shape, size, and placement is Amanda West's Best in Show winner of the early 1970s, Ch. Ralanda Ami Pierre. (Frasie photo)

Assignment

1. Make an appointment with the person in your breed or the breed you are studying who has developed a reputation through the years for producing dogs of outstanding quality. Have the person discuss and show you what he or she considers an outstanding head and *explain why* this is so.

2. Determine the overall shape that the standard of your breed requires, and see how well the heads of the dogs you look at fit that shape.

3. Determine where, within that shape, the ears, eyes, and nose should be located, and become familiar with their relative positions.

⑨ Movement

"Movement tells all," a tried and true axiom of those who appreciate fine dogs. It is important to understand that the movement must "tell all" about its own breed. Pictured is young Amy Rodrigues and her own Brittany in the classic Joan Ludwig photo of the dog in action.

*B*ack when I was still showing and breeding, I owned a wonderful Chow Chow bitch whose name was Blossom. She was a product of Joel Marston's Starcrest bloodline and the love of my life. Blossom possessed every characteristic that endears the breed to those who know Chow Chows well. She even added a few delightful quirks to the package that she had made up on her own.

Blossom was one of those one-in-a-million dogs who provided some of the happiest and some of the saddest moments of my life in dogs. She was, in fact, the subject of "Blossom Time," a story chronicling her life and death that I wrote many years ago and is considered a classic by many of our veteran Chow Chow lovers. In addition to her exceptional personality, Blossom was a pretty good representative of the breed.

Blossom wasn't shown much because she was housebroken. Now, that may sound like a peculiar thing to say, but when I say she was housebroken, I mean *exactly* that! Blossom relieved herself privately, behind a huge Camellia shrub at the farthest corner of our property—and *only* behind the huge Camellia shrub at the farthest corner of our property.

Yes, I was familiar with "matching" dogs back then, but while matching takes care of bowel problems it does nothing for the bladder, and Blossom would rather have passed on to doggy heaven before she would have been so indelicate as to attend to her toilette anywhere but in the privacy of her own home turf.

So, you can easily see that our show career was limited to those events we could get to and from in a matter of a few hours at most. Only those who know the greater Los Angeles area, where I was living at the time, can appreciate how severely that limits one's aspirations for a show career.

However, once a year there was a huge puppy match held within what could almost be considered walking distance of my home. Exhibitors often showed young dogs in puppy matches back then. Nowadays it appears people are too busy worrying about whether or not they're going to win the Group at Westminster to be concerned with such mundane things as a puppy match.

At any rate, I had Blossom in perfect coat and trained to a fare thee well, which, considering her flamboyant personality, was a genuine accomplishment! There were a number of Chow

Chows entered, and much to my delight my girl was placed Best of Breed. Group competition followed almost immediately afterward, so we stayed on.

It quickly became apparent that my competition was a beautiful young Lhasa Apso. The judge poked, prodded, and compared the two and finally had the two of us go around the ring together. The Lhasa streaked on ahead, golden tresses flying in the wind.

This was back in the days when John Thyssen was showing the fabulous Ch. Yojimbo's Orion, a dog capable of burning up the rings with his ground-covering movement. Therefore, *all* Lhasas were moved at that speed—capable or not.

As I had been carefully instructed by my Chow Chow mentors, I moved Blossom at the slow, steady pace that would produce that stilted movement that is a hallmark of the breed. The judge pondered a moment or two and then pointed—to the Lhasa.

"Oh well, it was a good one," I consoled myself (sort of!).

But then the judge made the fatal mistake of saying, "Your Chow is one of the nicest I've seen, but the Lhasa out-moved you today. You've got to teach your Chow to move out a bit."

Showing "Blossom," my first Chow Chow, put me in touch with the fact that all too often a dog is penalized for moving as its breed should. Blossom is pictured here with one of her best friends, Tom Roh. (Author photo)

To say I was furious would be an understatement! I don't think I've ever quite gotten over that, because to this day moving properly *for its breed* remains a significant factor in my evaluating breed type.

So, what's the big deal? It's a dog *show,* isn't it? What's wrong with some good old showmanship?

There's *nothing* wrong with showmanship, but showmanship is one thing, and...well, let's go on to our fourth element of breed type—movement, and the sins that are committed against correct movement day in and day out.

The three cardinal sins of movement

It's amazing how many things are included under movement that have little or nothing to do with it. Some are the result of minor misunderstandings, others are downright blunders. (As you might guess, I consider the dastardly "Blossom at the Puppy Match Incident" one of the latter!) Without a doubt, the three most damaging misunderstandings surrounding movement are:

1. Confusing correct movement with showmanship.
2. Believing the basic principles governing canine locomotion produce only one kind of movement.
3. Not understanding that changing movement changes type.

Let's take a look at each of these offenses and see not only why they are committed so frequently but their ultimate consequences as well.

No. 1 The first and most common offense perpetrated against movement is confusing correct movement with showmanship. One has little to do with the other. A very good dog can *show* poorly on any given day and still be *moving* properly. That is, the dog could care less about being there, but its legs are following a certain specified course and conducting themselves in the prescribed manner for that breed. On the other hand, a dog moving improperly could easily *love* being there and show its head off, but *it is not moving in the proper manner for its breed*. Guess which dog usually wins?

No. 2   The second sin committed against evaluating proper movement is made by insisting that because the basic principles that govern canine locomotion remain the same for all dogs, it then follows that all dogs will move in the same manner. Unfortunately, this is where the sound movement clinics can lead people astray. The problem is unintentional, I'm sure, but many students come away from seminars of this nature believing that there is only one kind of "sound" movement.

The manner in which a dog is *constructed* determines how the general rules governing canine locomotion are allowed to play themselves out. Yes, the rules of kinesiology and biomechanics apply to the Peke every bit as much as they do to the Borzoi. However, it is the individual construction of the two animals that determines how those rules come into play and each of them will consequently move. Some dogs have a rolling gait, others hackney, still others are short striding and stilted. They are all correct—*for their breed.*

No. 3   The third and most grievous of the cardinal sins against movement is not facing the fact that changing movement changes type! Type is what lends distinction to a breed. Should you have missed this message in what I've written so far, please go back to the first page of this book and start reading all over again—you've missed the very essence of everything I've written.

Judges who fault a dog for moving correctly for its breed should not be allowed in a ring. Breeders who cavalierly dispense with their breed's correct movement in pursuit of something more apt to bring home a greater number of blue ribbons should be banned from the ranks!

Perhaps that sounds somewhat extreme (and I'm the first to admit I may still be suffering the agony of poor Blossom's crushing defeat back those thousands of years ago); however, allowing breeds to move in a more "generally acceptable" or "more attractive" manner is an insidious situation that is leading us into that "generic landslide" I have so often spoken and written about.

Each breed should move in the manner that accommodates its structure and purpose

There's a bit more to correct movement than "down and back, please," or "take them around once more." All breeds of dogs are capable of doing either or both. However, the importance of what fulfilling those requests tells us is often ignored for the sake of the spectacular. Unlike seeing a dog live or in a video, "action" shots don't reveal many of the characteristic differences that will occur when the dog is moving properly for its breed.

Without a doubt, Sporting Dog movement is among the flashiest and glamorous of all breeds. Those who appreciate this movement should be aware that its essence is not in speed but in efficiency. Sporting Dogs must cover great distances over prolonged periods with a maximum of efficiency. Their reach and drive accommodates this. Although this movement is proper for dogs of the Sporting Group and at the same time attractive, it should not be superimposed on all breeds arbitrarily. (Pictured in the Russ Kinne photo is Colly Holmes' English Setter, Ch. Mysti's Triumph of Valley Run)

Although the breed standard includes reach and drive as typical of the Lakeland Terrier's gait, we are given much the same information about many breeds. What should be given particular notice are the standard's opening statements under General Appearance, which read in part, "The Lakeland Terrier was bred to hunt vermin in the rugged shale mountains of the Lake District of northern England....He has sufficient length of leg under him to cover rough ground easily.... His movement is lithe and graceful." This Terrier was bred to work in rugged terrain. Thus, flexibility and maneuverability, rather than dead-ahead speed, should be considered here. (Callea photo of a Black Watch Lakeland Terrier)

In the ring we are not able to test the Borzoi's maneuverability or the speed and endurance required to course wild game on open terrain. To further complicate matters, we evaluate this breed's movement at a trot although everything in the breed's development was aimed at performance on the open course. In order to properly evaluate correct movement in a coursing breed, an in-depth knowledge of correct coursing dog conformation is paramount. Limited to in-ring observation, any restrictive or unsound movement that would impair the breed's speed or athleticism must be particularly penalized. The Callea photo of Ch. Kishniga Desert Song is an excellent example of what the well-made Borzoi gives us in motion.

172   Solving the Mysteries of Breed Type

The Old English Sheepdog worked as a drover's dog—driving sheep and cattle from the rural areas of England to city markets. Months were invested in fattening the livestock in order to enhance their market value. Therefore, getting them to their destination had to be done in a calm, slow-paced manner so they would not worry their weight away. The Old English Sheepdog was able to do just that, with its easygoing way of moving "covering maximum ground with minimum steps...(seen to) amble or pace at slower speeds." The breed should exhibit this same demeanor and qualities of movement today. This classic photo of Mona Berkowitz and one her many outstanding Old English Sheepdogs portrays the essence of the breed's movement. (Jayne Langdon photo)

The Australian Cattle Dog was bred for one of the toughest jobs its country had to offer—that of minding and rounding up the half-wild cattle of Australia's vast ranches (or "stations," as they are called "down under"). History, purpose, and today's standard emphasize the qualities that equip the Australian Cattle Dog to do so. "Soundness is of paramount importance. The action is true, free, supple and tireless. The movement of the shoulders and forelegs with the powerful thrust of the hindquarters in unison. Capability of quick and sudden [m]ovement is essential." Every step this breed takes should speak for its origin and purpose. (Jayne Langdon photo)

Chapter 9 Movement 173

The English Toy Spaniel traces its ancestry to both a Toy and Spaniel source. It must adhere to the physical limitations placed on all members of the Toy Group, along with the pleasant, perky attitude of the dog bred to please. The breed must do so without betraying the soundness of construction and movement inherited from its Spaniel ancestors. Thus, its movement is "elegant...free and lively, evidencing stable character and correct construction...resulting from straight boned fronts and properly made and muscled hindquarters." It's quite clear what those involved with the breed must keep in mind when evaluating movement. Ch. Dreamridge Dear Daphne illustrates what her breed is capable of when adhering to the designs of the standard. (Callea photo)

International concern

Movement as it affects type isn't a problem peculiar to American dogs or even a purely Western phenomenon—it prevails throughout the dog world. It creates concern particularly among breeders and judges who have been around long enough to have been influenced by dog fanciers who appreciated—make that *prized*—the uniqueness of our breeds.

Hans Lehtinen and Chris Lummelampi are two highly respected all-around judges who reside in Finland. The former has probably judged at every important dog show in the world with the exception of our Westminster Kennel Club, which normally restricts its panel to domestic judges.

The decisions of the two are held in high regard wherever they have passed judgment. Together Lehtinen and Lummelampi wrote of the movement and type relationship to which I refer in a 1996 edition of England's outstanding weekly newspaper, *Dog World*.

"Movement is a measure of a dog's conformation. If we accept what might be today's barely perceptible changes in a breed's movement, we may gradually allow an alteration in breed type. We may, in fact, contribute to a situation where an Afghan Hound moves like a Poodle and a Poodle moves like an Afghan. If this is the case then we need a serious discussion on typical movement in today's show rings.

"In some breeds, function dictates movement. In others, there does not seem much logical explanation why a breed should move in a certain way except when the movement is part of the breed's heritage and deserves recognition."

The two writers go on to lament the loss of the Fox Terrier's movement in which the forelegs move like the pendulum of a clock, the "bustling" action of the English Cocker Spaniel, the true hackney of the Miniature Pinscher, the "rolling" gait of the Clumber due its long body and short legs.

Can we be so naive as to believe for a single moment that changing what permitted these mandated styles of movement will not change the manner in which the breeds are constructed? Or that dogs bred to move about at a plodding or even sensible rate of speed are not going to be changed by an ability to move out like a launched rocket?

Chapter 9 Movement 175

Changing movement changes type

The photographs of German Shepherd Ch. Altana's Mystique (above) and Chow Chow Ch. Black Panther of Cad (below) illustrate the vast difference in type and construction that is correct for the two breeds. Maximum angulation allows German Shepherd Dog Ch. Altana's Mystique to move at a flying trot. The restricted angulation required of the Chow Chow gives the breed its short-strided and stilted gait. The only way to make the Chow Chow move with the German Shepherd's extended trot would be to change the construction of the breed's front and rear quarter. And for the benefit of those who have not had much breeding experience, it is important to understand that you do not change one part of a dog's anatomy without it affecting the adjacent bones. (Mystique appears in a Cook photo and Black Panther in a Missy photo)

There is no doubt in my mind that a good part of all this is the result of the emphasis we've placed on "the big wins" of the day—Groups and Bests in Show. There it takes a certain degree of glamour and charisma to draw the ringside into the proceedings. The fast dog—hair flying in all directions—is a lot more spectacular and has more crowd appeal and, granted, may be entirely correct *for some breeds.*

Admittedly, it has to be difficult for the exhibitors of the less flashy breeds to constantly play bridesmaid to the more glamorous brides of the canine world. Still, I think the breeder earns a great deal more respect from those who really know dogs when they stay on purpose and remain loyal to the intent of their breed.

To the fastest go the spoils

There is too great an inclination to use the same yardstick to measure quality in vastly different breeds. One of those measurements is speed. For whatever the reason, exhibitors seem to think speed is an essential of a top-winning show dog. It makes so little sense, and yet one would be led to believe that if you can get a Bulldog to move (as I've heard so often) "like a German Shepherd," you have a better Bulldog. If a German Shepherd's movement is what you want, perhaps getting a German Shepherd would be the thing to do. Or so it seems to me.

It is up to the exhibitor to know the proper speed at which to move a dog and the judge's responsibility to keep the dogs in the ring moving at a pace most suitable for the breed. A dog forced to move beyond its proper speed will begin to exhibit faults that may or may not be there.

Our obsession with winning Groups and all-breed Bests in Show puts us in constant danger of all of our breeds converging toward a commonality—of sharing those glamorous characteristics that put a dog across when the going gets tough but which at the same time are contrary to the breed's character and conformation. I appreciate the dog who sells himself as much as the next guy, but do we want and need the Bulldog to bounce around like the Poodle or the Basset Hound to streak out ahead of the Afghan Hound?

Understand, this is not a condemnation of any of the Best-in-Show-winning characteristics I have mentioned, as long as they are appropriate for the breed. Not all breeds were meant to move in a flamboyant fashion.

There's no greater eye appeal than that of the Afghan, Irish Setter, or German Shepherd as they move around the ring. It's "showbiz" at its best. Attractive and flashy? Yes. Universally correct—*absolutely not!*

There is no way on God's green earth that we are going to be able to get that kind of movement out of a correctly made French Bulldog, or for that matter any of the Terrier breeds, short legged or long. When any breed begins to drift toward generic movement, as subtle as that drift may initially be, other changes begin to take place, and these changes affect breed type.

There are those who refer to exhibiting purebred dogs a sport. For some it is, but the danger in doing so exists when all dogs are referred to as "efficient athletes." In some breeds, function dictates movement. In others, the term "athlete" does not apply at all. Some of our breeds were never intended to be athletic, nor can their correct manner of movement even be considered efficient. For instance, neither the high lift of the Italian Greyhound's movement (left) nor the "hackney" movement of the proper Miniature Pinscher (right) is remotely related to efficiency. Their movement is for artistic effect as much as it is in the hackney gait of the horse, and it is an important part of the two breeds' type. Eliminating or refining this movement for the sake of efficiency or athleticism would be no less a error than robbing the Sporting dog of its ground-covering reach and drive.

Change for change's sake

Having the Basset Hound move with the rapid-fire reach and drive of a Sighthound can only be accomplished in one way—by straightening the front legs. First, it must be understood that the Basset Hound was created to be a plodding, slow-paced hunting dog that the hunter could easily follow and keep up with. In order to accomplish this, the creators of the breed bred for construction that would achieve this end. The extremely short legs that wrap around the body and restrict movement were and are correct for the breed.

I have always wondered why it is that people will become attracted to a breed, and as soon as they become involved, set about changing it in some way. They get a Sighthound and want it to act like a Poodle or a reasonably coated breed and want to grow coat that comes to the floor. Why not get a breed that already has what they want and leave the other breeds as they were intended to be?

The drifts and slides are not always as extreme as some I've mentioned. Often they are far more subtle but nonetheless important. Take, for instance, the case of the Gordon and Irish Setters. Few can argue the glamour and excitement created by the Irish Setter's flashy ground-covering movement. The breed moves as it does because of what it was created to do in the field. The Irishman has (or should have) that sleek whip-cord look in keeping with the job he has to do.

The purpose of the Gordon Setter, on the other hand, was much different than that of its Irish cousin. The Gordon worked on the rocky, frequently inhospitable terrain of the Scottish Highlands. Care and deliberation in movement were important to the breed. Racing headlong across the moors could prove extremely dangerous to the feet and legs of the breed, to say nothing of the poor hunter's ability to keep up with the dog. Thus, the Scots bred to create a dog who was shorter coupled, heavier bodied, and slower moving than the fleet and lithe Irishman. (Here's that good old "horses for courses" again!)

That speedy, slenderized, "elegant," and much faster version of the Gordon appears more and more often in today's show rings. Regrettably, unless the protests of the die-hards in the breed are loud enough and adamant enough, this drift is a portent of things to come.

Those wanting or expecting Irish Setter movement should look to the Irish Setter and not the Gordon. Here again, I must ask, isn't it our responsibility as breeders and judges to honor the intent and purpose of the breed?

Those who taught me led me to believe that very often it is tradition itself that maintains a standard in dog breeds. I guess those of us from the old school have to get wise to the fact that new traditions do arise, but any self-respecting dog man and woman will experience a twinge of heart when the new traditions cancel out those things that have historically been considered hallmarks of a breed. Things such as the movement that is often unique to a single breed.

Although some of the "new" Havanese fanciers of America will surely challenge me every step of the way, I live in wonder as to the how and why of the peculiar additions and revisions to the breed's standard. A hallmark of all the Bichon breeds (Bolognaise, Havanese, and Frise) for nearly one hundred years has been the athletic, easy, get-out-of-the-way-quickly kind of movement the breeds share. Now the Havanese is asked to move toward the observer flapping, or as referred to in the new standard, *flashing* its front feet high enough so that the pads of the feet will be easily visible!

I have judged the Havanese abroad and frequently here in the United States for many years prior to its AKC recognition. I cannot recall seeing the movement called for in the current AKC standard of the breed. I cannot say that it does not exist anywhere other than here in the United States, but I can say that the currently described movement requires an anatomically different kind of dog than that which I have judged previously. That said, it appears that this is movement so desired by the parent club, and this is what judges must abide by.

Then and now

Granted, two different worlds are yesterday and today. Back in those good-old-bad-old days (when I was the thoroughly modern one and everyone else an old fuddy-duddy!), those irascible old judges we showed under would have turned us over to the SPCA before they would have allowed us to do such things as even hint at stringing up our dogs. A dog moving out in front on the end of slightly taut lead was about as far as we could get with those old-timers, and that was on their kinder days.

We took a great deal of pride in the fact that our dogs could perform on their own, in their distinct manner and at their own rate of speed. I still find movement that is normal to the breed both attractive and important to the essence of the breed.

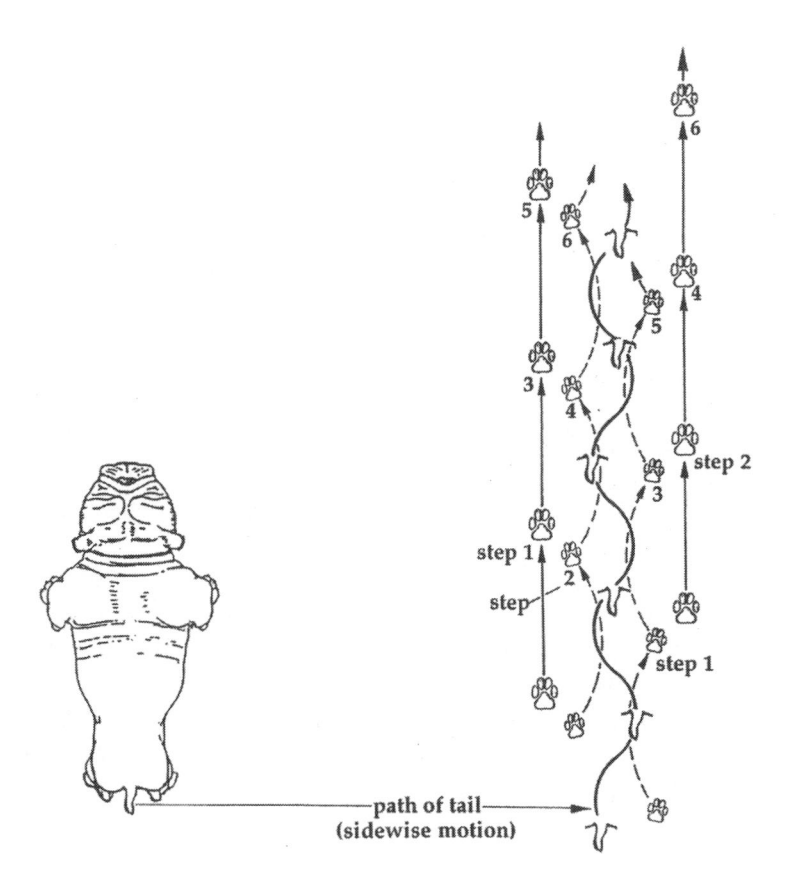

The Bulldog Club of America is responsible for one of the finest educational programs in pure-bred dogs. Its devoted officers and committee heads offer educational events that deal with all aspects of breed type. The accompanying illustration of Bulldog gait is a sample of the detail available to the Bulldog student. It is taken from the Bulldog Club of America's educational brochure and appears here with the club's approval.

Assignment

1. Observe your breed or the new breed you are studying to determine which characteristics of movement are unique to the breed.

2. Research the standard, origin, and history for written and unwritten clues as to what is or should be distinctive about the breed's movement.

3. Speak to successful veteran breeders for their input in regard to the above.

4. After you have completed Steps 1-3, observe the breed again, noting which of these characteristics have been maintained, which have been lost or are in danger of being lost, and finally make special note of those things in the breed's movement that are in conflict with what you have determined is important.

5. What physical changes assist the perpetuation of these undesirable movement traits?

10 Coat

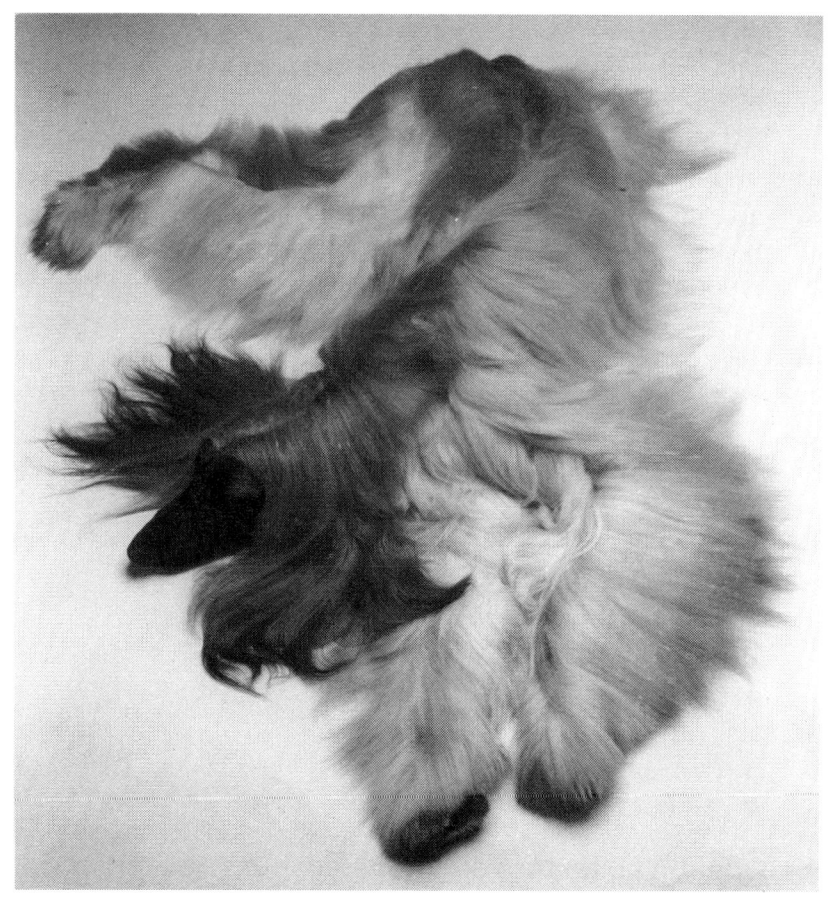

Leo Tolstoy wrote, " It is amazing how complete is the delusion that beauty is goodness." And how guilty we in dogs are of being deluded by this crowning glory our breeds. In the end we must ask ourselves, "Is the dog wearing the coat, or is the coat wearing the dog?" Pictured is Afghan Hound Ch. Sakkhara's Pharaoh.

Something I find interesting is how often the same exhibitors who have no qualms about showing dogs that are out of condition—too fat or too thin—or even dogs that are unsound, wouldn't *think* about showing a dog that is out of coat. The same old saw applies here, of course—if some is good, ten times more is better.

It's also interesting to note that if a standard even hints at the fact that the breed should be "well coated," you can rest assured that nine times out of ten, the words will be interpreted to mean *amount*, and not a whole lot more.

Amount of hair and how it's trimmed are extremely important in today's penchant for the glamour dogs. In truth, they are an important part of type in a good many of our breeds. But what seems to get lost in the translation from standard to execution is that amount of coat and the way that coat is trimmed are only a part of what coat is all about—and in some breeds a very small part. A very obvious part, granted, but only a small part of what we must consider as breeders and judges.

Coat, as we will deal with it here—and as it should be dealt with in the ring and in breeding programs—includes all of its aspects:

- Serviceability
- Texture
- Quality
- Pattern
- Color
- Trim
- Distribution
- Amount

Serviceability, texture and quality

Most standards for the utility breeds describe a coat that assists the dog in performance of its duty. Function then becomes a very important part of type—no less a consideration in that aspect than the Bull Terrier's head or the Dalmatian's markings. There is nothing about type that says what is asked for in respect to coat must be exotic in nature. It is how much the characteristic defines the breed that dictates its importance.

An Alaskan Malamute with long silky hair and no undercoat would be disqualified forever insofar as its ability to work. Consider what would happen to the Malamute gone astray in the Arctic environment wearing that kind of coat. Chances of survival would be narrowed considerably if not entirely eliminated. Those who claim devotion to the breed have elected to make blue eyes the sole disqualification and tell the breeder and judge to penalize the poor coat to the extent of its departure from the ideal. This depends entirely upon the observer's ability to understand what proper texture and quality really is. Thus, it becomes contingent upon the breed's parent club to exercise all efforts to educate thoroughly in this respect.

Undoubtedly, in some minds this brings up the old caveat about our dogs no longer being forced to endure circumstances of such a drastic nature as they might have at their inception. I have stated it before and will say it again—there is absolutely no rationalization that justifies making any dog a misfit or incapable of serving the purpose for which it was developed simply to please our own egos.

Must a breed continue to serve in its original purpose? I would venture to say the dog would probably be happiest doing so, but that is not always possible. Robbing the breed of its ability to do so, however, is not within our right as dog breeders or as judges.

Here again, I must caution our judges who approach their task with a generous desire to assist highly campaigned dogs in achieving their lofty goals. Such benevolence may bring one to overlook critical points such as these in discussion at extreme detriment to the breed. Kindness, consideration, and assistance are options open to the judge only to the extent they serve the breed.

Field dog breeders continually stress the importance of maintaining the serviceability of their breeds. Our Herding breeds are given more and more opportunity to exercise their inherited abilities. Breeders are becoming ever more aware that dogs able to perform the tasks for which their ancestors were developed are far better for the experience.

I seriously doubt that those who allow their water-retrieving breeds to work would bother with dogs whose coats are of a texture that would absorb and hold water: certainly one of the most grievous faults that dogs of this purpose could have.

Yet, entirely incorrect coats are not only overlooked by judges, exhibitors spend long hours and young fortunes on products that remove the very essence of what makes the coat correct. Stop by the Retriever grooming areas just before show time. No, those aren't Poodles under the hair dryers and clouds of chalk.

I have had judges react in disgust because their Chesapeake Bay Retriever entries had oily coats (proper for the breed). These soil their hands, but the same judges clap their lily-white hands in glee and rush to reward the coats scrubbed until they are entirely robbed of their oils and texture and then blown dry to a puffed-up fare thee well. In both the Canadian and American Chessie Standards' Scale of Points, the highest count is given to coat and texture.

So here we go again with origin and purpose. We have dogs that were created with a specific working purpose in mind. Their coats were developed to allow the dog to perform at its best: in the water, through brush, or across desert sands.

There are so many poorly coated dogs of the various breeds being shown—and winning—that the incorrect coat has become the norm and the properly coated dog is penalized for its "difference." Think about that one for a bit.

The proper harsh Schnauzer coat has been traded off for abundance, and abundance calls for softer and silkier. A veteran Miniature Schnauzer breeder only recently observed, "Thank the Lord our breed has cropped ears. If they had long ears, we wouldn't be able to tell them from American Cockers!"

As I said previously, all breeds were created with a purpose in mind, whether that purpose was serviceability or beauty. In the case of the latter, coat texture holds just as important a place as it does for the utility breeds, albeit for much different reasons.

The sweeping silken tresses of the Yorkshire Terrier and the Maltese are as much a part of their breed type as is the Chesapeake's "waved-not-curled-hair," as Anne Rogers Clark described it so aptly in her discussion of the breed.

The proper herding breeds' coats were developed to do nothing if not protect the dogs. Something tells me the dog wearing the proper Old English coat while out guarding his flock would not be that giant ball of fluff we see in the ring today. It would be of such a nature that wind and rain and pounding storms would turn it into a well-matted and tangled suit of armor that would help the dog withstand any rain, sleet, and blinding snowstorm.

Should the Old English be shown matted and tangled? Of course not. Should the breed have the correct coat that would do just that if needed? It must to be correct! It remains with us to breed that kind of coat and to reward that kind of coat as judges.

So, what am I advocating? That we show our dogs matted and unclean? Not at all. The point that I attempt to make is that we respect, as part of breed type, the coats that actually do typify the breeds.

Coats grow in and fall out, only to grow in again. There are so many products on the market to encourage hair growth, it's become a whole industry. It is indeed rare to find dogs in the ring today that don't have lots of it. Now, when it comes to the proper coat, and I do mean the real texture—not that which comes from some bottle or can—well, that's a different matter.

Pattern and distribution

Few people stop to give much thought to why standards ask for certain kinds of hair to be placed in certain specified areas of a breed. The Collie standard's statement, "coat is very abundant on the mane and frill," was undoubtedly less for the dramatic effect than for the fact that it protected the vital organs of this clever herding breed.

Something tells me that the Beardie's "coat increases in length towards the chest, forming the typical beard" might have had as much to do with protection as it did with providing the breed with the distinctive beard.

The Poodle's clip (as exotic as it has become) comes from early attempts to protect the breed's "action parts" from freezing waters. Note how well the huge ruff protects vital organs. Each of those fancy "bracelets" wraps around the Poodle's joints. The trim is as functional as the coat's texture. It is there to *protect*.

The Labrador Retriever's unique and distinct otter tail is a matter of both construction and pattern. It stems from purpose, making the Lab one of the best water retrieving Sporting Dogs in existence. The tail is an efficient rudder, and the hair of the tail wraps and protects that valuable navigational tool.

There are countless patterns called for throughout the standards, and it is up to those pursuing knowledge of a breed to ferret this information—not just to be aware that the characteristic may be called for, but also why it is called for.

Color

Some breed standards go so far as to say "any color allowed" or "a good dog can't be a bad color." This does not apply in all cases. In fact, in some breeds, correct color constitutes a part of a breed's correct type—sometimes simply through tradition and at other times through both tradition and purpose.

Proper color is, of course, a part of what helps distinguish the three Setters, but color also helps a dog perform in many cases. The colors called for in the Chesapeake standard ("Any color of brown, sedge or deadgrass") allows the dog to move about in perfect camouflage.

The Border Collie's white flashes (muzzle, collar, chest and feet, and tail tip) certainly made keeping track of the those black dogs much easier as they brought the flocks together during winter's early nightfalls. Not so stupid, those stockmen of old!

The Sussex Spaniel standard reads: "Color—Rich golden liver is the *only* acceptable color and is a certain sign of the purity of the breed. Dark liver or puce is a major fault." The italics are mine to highlight a very important and all-too-often entirely ignored word.

The Samoyed's coat "should glisten with a silver sheen," and we know that the Yorkie's body coat should be "a dark steel-blue, not a silver-blue and not mingled with fawn, bronzy or black hairs." The Soft Coated Wheaten Terrier standard is emphatic that "the overall coloring must clearly be wheaten with no evidence of any other color except on ears and muzzle where blue-gray shading is sometimes present."

Black Pugs and Chow Chows never seem to have the proper wrinkling their lighter colored counterparts have, but a good part of that can be the absence of contrast. Lighter colors show the nuances of shading. Black does not offer that opportunity. Therefore, very close examination is necessary.

Markings

Breeders who come from breeds of more than one color are keenly aware of the great impact markings can have optically. My specialty in Cockers was the parti-color variety, so I need no reminder to pay very close attention to what lies beneath those markings—some of which can all but destroy a dog's opportunities in the show ring.

The English Springer Spaniel can have body markings that slant back along the shoulder, creating an illusion of beautiful shoulder angulation when in fact the shoulder might be set all but vertically. On the other hand, the most beautifully laid-back shoulder can appear poker straight with an unfortunate shoulder marking.

The actual markings are of little consequence in the English Springer Spaniel insofar as the observer doesn't mistake any distortion they might create for a fault of construction. On the other hand, markings do constitute an element of type in other breeds. The Papillon standard gives sufficient detail about how and where color should appear on the white background to make markings something that must be included in our consideration of type.

Facial markings lacking symmetry can create all kinds of strange illusions. Tan facial markings on standard bi-colored dogs can make or break an expression, depending upon amount and placement. Familiarity with the breed standard and close examination are required to avoid being led astray in our summation. Some standards, such as that of the Pointer, concede nothing to color; but when a standard details its color specifications, it becomes abundantly clear that we who breed and judge have no options if we are going to reward type. Settling for less allows our decisions to stray from type. It is our responsibility as breeders and judges to respect these distinguishing characteristics and include them in our summary of this element of breed type.

Trim

If there is anything we have mastered here in North America, it is the ability to grow hair and trim it well. Nowhere—and I've traveled the world comparing—nowhere has the art of dog grooming been developed to such a high degree as it has in the United States. Unfortunately, in too many cases we've come to value our accomplishment to such a degree that it takes precedence over all other factors that constitute excellence in coat quality.

In order for an exhibitor to win regularly with breeds such as the Bichon Frise, Cocker Spaniel, or Poodle, the person must be able to groom the dog at a level comparable to the breed's true experts. So it is, and if the amateur wants to remain competitive, he or she must be able to master the art.

Breed experts may be able to look past this cosmetic expertise to see what lies beneath, but unfortunately, too many others cannot. Fortunately, however, it is rare that the best dogs in these breeds are given the benefit of ideal presentation. The fact remains that breeders and judges must not allow themselves to be misled by scissor work—clever or otherwise.

The groomer's art is probably more apt to seduce those who come from the smooth breeds than those who have been forced to learn the tricks of the trade in their own coated breeds. In the smooth breeds, what's there is there for all to see. In the coated breeds, there are countless options and illusions that can be resorted to. The groomer can cut away the undesirables or add what is missing—or so it appears. Trimming gilds the lily and sometimes the dandelion.

When first judging the coated breeds, those who have not had grooming experience may have to rely solely upon their hands until they train themselves to see through and recognize what lies beneath the hair. Scissors can disguise but only *disguise* and not change what is there. Scissors do not change the dog, only the hair of the dog. It is up to the observer to find what in fact is really there. A good question to ask is, "Is the dog wearing the coat, or is the coat wearing the dog?"

A lot of hair on top of a Bichon's head or trimming that neck line to extend down along the Bichon's back is not what constitutes a long neck. The only thing that makes for a long neck is proper length of the neck itself and a well laid-back shoulder.

A well-trimmed and presented dog is a thing of beauty, but it must be understood that its appearance is largely dependent upon the skill of the groomer—the dog sporting that trim has no genes to pass on for good grooming.

Assessing grooming also includes assessing those breeds that are not to be clipped or trimmed and even those that allow little or no neatening or shaping. The latter are an even greater challenge to evaluate, but here again, their casual presentation is thought to be a part of their respective breed's type.

The General Appearance paragraph of the breed standard for the Cavalier King Charles Spaniel clearly states, "natural appearance with no trimming, sculpting or artificial alteration is essential to breed type." To make sure the breeder and judge have not missed that statement or underestimated its importance, under "Coat," the standard goes on to say, "Specimens where the coat has been altered by trimming, clipping, or by artificial means shall be so severely penalized as to be effectively eliminated from competition." (The standard does allow the hair growing between the pads on the underside of the feet to be trimmed.)

Here, then, trimming—or perhaps better stated, the prohibition of any trimming—becomes a clearly defined part of the essence of the Cavalier. The natural state of the coat is no less an element of breed type than the Irish Setter's "Mahogany or rich chestnut red" color or the "oil in the harsh outer coat and woolly undercoat" of the Chesapeake Bay Retriever. These are not elements that can be dismissed in favor of enhancement in the pursuit of blue ribbons or Bests in Show.

Amount

What can be said about amount of hair that hasn't been said here and a million times over elsewhere? There is a proper amount of coat for each and every breed, but one would think we were fanciers of sheep rather than dogs in the value we place on amount.

I think we have to accept the fact that if the exhibitor can grow it, he or she will grow it. It is very much a personal opinion, but I believe that all other factors in evaluating hair considered, amount would be the least of my concerns. What we are apt to consider an insufficient amount of coat today is probably more than twice that considered adequate in the founders' original concept.

What does "well-coated" mean?

If you were to take inventory of all the words devoted to coat in the standards of our AKC breeds, the tally would probably be huge. On the other hand, if you were to judge by which of those words receives the most attention, it would seem that just one had any real importance. That one word is—amount. Ironically, of all the factors this element of breed type involves, amount is the one our breeds are in least danger of falling short of.

The American Cocker takes a great deal of criticism for the amount of coat the breed carries. Actually, coat is a problem that can be dispensed with quite easily through the judicious use of a pair of scissors. Of greater concern should be the texture of the mammoth coats we see on the dogs today. The origin and purpose of the Cocker, like it is for all sporting Spaniels, lies in field work. The hard-surfaced, silky texture of the correct Spaniel coat allows thorns and brambles to slide away. In far too many cases, coats have deteriorated considerably over the years. Prior to the 1960s, the Cocker was presented in a trim that allowed the observer to see what the dog's legs were doing in movement. The texture of that coat was indeed Spaniel. According to the standard, "silky, flat or slightly wavy and of a texture which permits easy care. Excessive coat or curly or cottony textured coat shall be severely penalized." Annette Davies's Ch. Feinlyne Femme Fatale typifies what the standard asks for as she's pictured winning Best of Variety at the 1957 Westminster Kennel Club show under judge Walter Tuddenham. (William Brown photo)

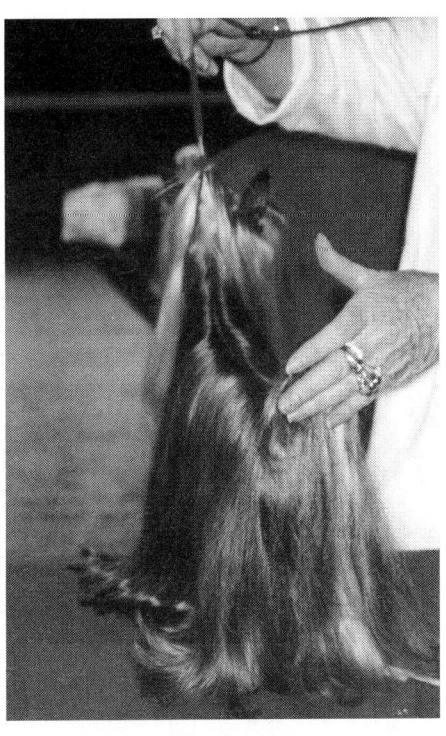

Spaniel coats derive their importance and become an element of type through function. The Yorkshire Terrier's metallic-colored coat is a unique and distinctive point of beauty. It is a type-defining element of this breed, whose purpose is to please. The standard of the breed stresses this element in saying, "Quality, texture and quantity of coat are of prime importance. Hair is glossy, fine and silky in texture." (Photo courtesy of Gerri Grieg)

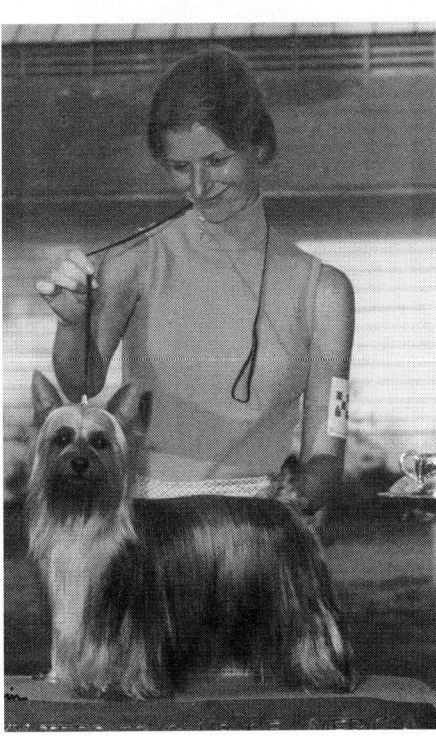

The Silky Terrier borrows much from its English cousin the Yorkshire Terrier in coat texture and color, but its standard gives a more serviceable image to the breed, with restrictions on amount and location of those important silken tresses. Color, shading, texture, amount, and location are all very important considerations in evaluating this element of type in the Silky Terrier. Pictured here is Florence Male's Ch. Weeblu's Trailblazer of Don-El, ROMX winning the 1980 National Specialty under judge R. Steven Shaw. (Jayne Langdon photo)

194 Solving the Mysteries of Breed Type

The proper harsh Schnauzer coat is too often relinquished in favor of abundance—abundance, unfortunately, calling for something softer and silkier. Would the spectacular silhouette and correct coat of Quintus v. Bergherbus, a European Giant Schnauzer, overcome his lack of furnishings were he competing in America today? (Shlomit photo)

Coats differentiate Chow Chows Ch. Wah-Hu Redcloud Sugar Daddy (rough) and Tamarin Red Velvet Foon Ying (smooth). Their coats must be evaluated within their own context, but the conformation of dogs of both coats remains exactly the same. In Chow Chows, both coats hold their own, and no concessions need to be made for either. In other breeds, however, the quality level may not be as equal, and the dogs at a lesser state are given priority because they may be the best that have come along. The important question to be asked in cases of this nature is whether making concessions assists or delays improvement. (Dennis Valadez photo)

Most people look at the Collie's coat as purely a thing of beauty; about this there is little argument. However, the fact that the coat is most abundant in the areas of the dog's vital organs can certainly be no accident. Origin and purpose tell us otherwise. (Ewing & Marlene Nicholson's beautifully coated Ch. Windarla's World Seeker is pictured here winning Group First under judge Richard D. Renihan (JD photo)

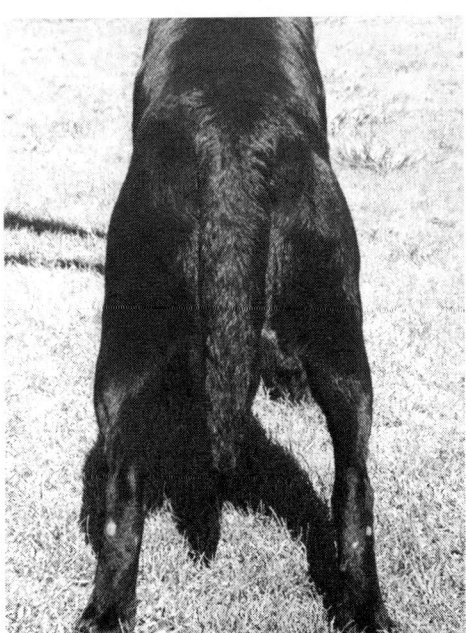

We find another example of coat pattern and serviceability coming into play in the tail of the Labrador Retriever. This is an obscure point in some other breeds, but here the unique manner in which the coat wraps and protects the tail of the water-retrieving Labrador becomes an important aspect of evaluating this element of breed type. The "otter" tail of the Lab serves as a rudder as it performs in the manner for which the breed was developed. Thus, a functional element becomes a point of excellence in evaluating this breed. (Linda Anderson photo)

196 *Solving the Mysteries of Breed Type*

The only difference in these three Spaniels is their markings. They are constructed, and their proportions are, exactly the same. Markings can deceive the observer. Therefore, close inspection of what lies beneath is extremely important. Although attractive markings have esthetic value in many breeds, unless they are specified in the breed standard, they should have no bearing on evaluating the quality of the dogs. That said, breeds such as Boston Terriers, Black and Tan American Cocker Spaniels, Mantle Great Danes, and Pembroke Welsh Corgis are required by merit of their standards to have markings in specified places.

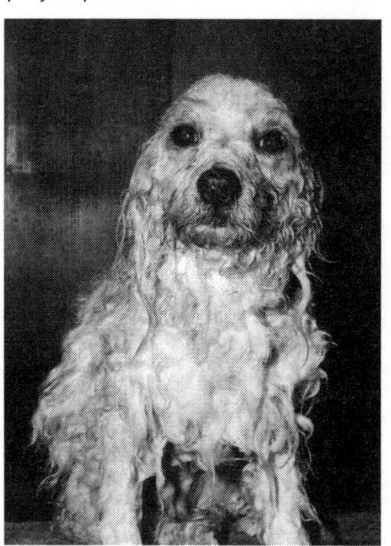

Trim and amount of coat play an extremely important role in the presentation of many breeds. Leaving too much on or cutting away too much can make faults appear that may not be there at all. On the other hand, clever scissors can enhance what may be missing. Neither breeders nor judges should allow themselves to be misled by the hair of the dog. Ch. Chaminade Mr. Beau Monde is pictured with his coat wet down (left) and as he normally appears (right). (Missy photos)

Chapter 10 Coat 197

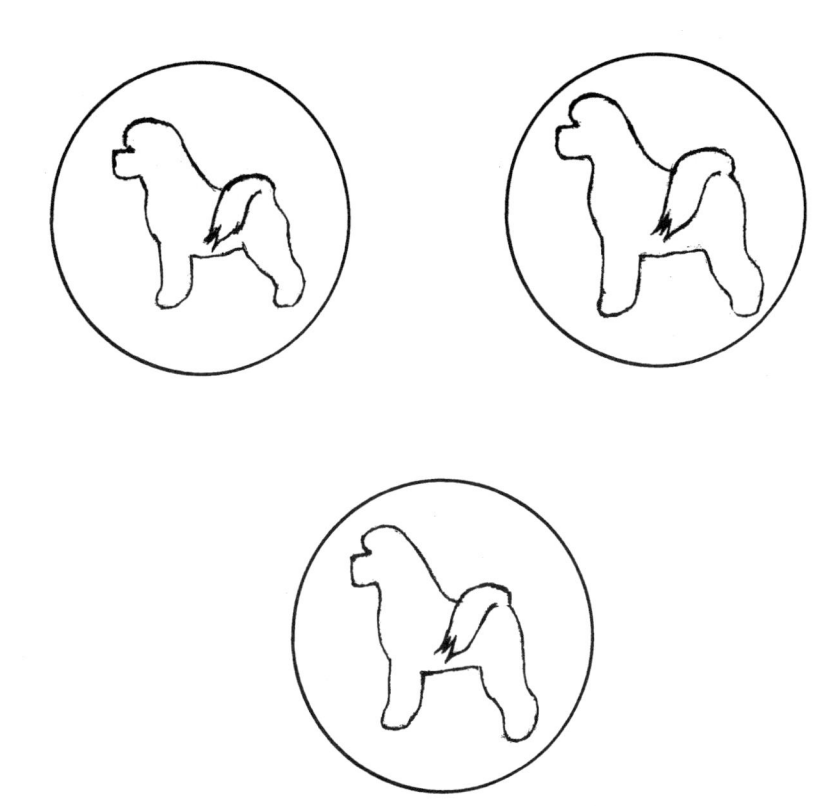

The standard of the Bichon Frise calls for a dog whose body length (sternum to buttocks) is a maximum of one-quarter longer than the dog is tall. It is of medium leg (withers to elbow representing 50 percent and elbow to ground representing 50 percent of the dog's total height). Which of these three dogs—dogs A (top left), B (top right), or C (bottom center)—might best represent those proportions? These same three dogs are pictured in Chapter 11 without their coats.

Assignment

1. Find out as much as you can about the kind of coat the origin and purpose of your breed dictated. Do not disregard doing so because a breed is considered purely decorative. In the vast majority of cases this characteristic is easily as important as it is to type in the utility breeds.

2. Based upon origin, purpose, and what the standard currently says, write down as complete a description as you can of that kind of coat.

3. Compare what you have written to the coats of the dogs you see in the ring.

4. Write down where in general the breed succeeds and where it fails in regard to the elements that constitute proper coat for the breed.

Part III
Applying Your Knowledge

11 The Breed-type Workbook

All give some, but there are some who give all. Champion Rimskittle Ruffian gave us all—always. Bred by Mr. & Mrs. James H. Clark, Ruffian is pictured here with handler Tim Brazier in a most remarkable Callea photo.

$\mathcal{B}$efore we began our journey through the essentials of breed type, I did my best to make it clear that no one has the ability to *teach* someone to recognize this elusive concept. That is something that only the student himself or herself can accomplish. However, I did say that a better understanding of just what breed type includes allows us to shed light on what otherwise might remain a vague and mysterious term forever. Hopefully, the information included in the preceding chapters has begun that process for you.

There is no doubt in my mind that anyone, even the beginning student of dogs, can learn to recognize type once he or she masters the components that combine to create it. Once these elements—the ones I like to call "The Big Five"—are understood, it becomes easy to understand why a dog must score well in each in order to qualify as an example of outstanding type.

Excellence in head or movement or any one aspect of type does not make the ideal dog. We can appreciate a dog for any single outstanding quality it might have, but the essence of type never lies in just one aspect of the total picture. This is something that applies whether evaluation takes place in the show ring, whelping box, or drawing board.

Entirely ignoring or, on the other hand, placing excessive emphasis on only one or two elements of type does great disservice to a breed, and the practice is certainly not what the student, or for that matter the veteran, should fall prey to. Let's take a look at how erring in either of these respects might affect a breed by using the popular Labrador Retriever as an example.

The Labrador Retriever has maintained its popularity as a triple-threat dog for decades. Our Lab friend—yellow, black, and chocolate—can be at once hunter, show dog, and family pal. Labrador Retriever entries, particularly at Specialty shows, are often among our strongest. It's a breed that captures the devotion of its fans and seemingly never lets go.

The enormous popularity of the breed gives dedicated breeders a huge burden of responsibility. Supplying quality puppies to meet the demands of the public is the only way well-bred, typical puppies will continue to represent the breed.

As long as entries remain high, judges will have to remain alert so that drifts and trends don't allow this well-established breed to veer off course. Let's see how this might occur by noting how too little or too much emphasis placed on one area of type or another can create distinct problems for the breed.

The generic landslide

Let me preface what will follow by saying that most anyone who has heard anything at all about Labs from a breeder will have heard that "head, coat, and tail" are considered of major consequence. No argument there—they *are* distinguishing characteristics. But let's get on with our example.

The generic approach to Lab evaluation would look for those "good old sportin' dog" basics—soundness of limb, easy ground-covering movement, correct color, good attitude, few failings with no major faults or disqualifications. The general picture would probably be one of a serviceable-looking dog who, when asked to, could and would be willing to put in a good day's work in the field.

This fellow is a good dog, but is he a good Labrador Retriever? Selecting the purely generic dog on the basis of overall Sporting Dog characteristics could easily bypass three of type's five basic elements—head, coat, and tail. The breed's tail in this instance actually combines two of the elements—silhouette and coat. The Lab tail is a part of what creates the breed's distinctive silhouette; a silhouette, mind you, that is fashioned by origin and purpose.

The silhouette of a well-made specimen of the breed is identifiable a mile off. (Well, perhaps not *a mile*, but you get my message, I'm sure.) His center of gravity falls a bit below that of his fellow Retrievers, but not so much that he wouldn't be able to jump a fence or clear the sides of a boat. And that tail—no other breed has one quite like the Lab's.

With the kind of construction required to create the proper silhouette, a Lab will move in a four-square manner. I say this in the sense that with proper body and bone and the accompanying body capacity, he will move in a resolute fashion—enduring rather than fast, owning the ground rather than cutting the air.

The Lab's head construction must be such that it enables him to do his work—strength without coarseness, moderation in every respect. The Lab's expression must reveal the kindness and gentleness the breed is appreciated for around the world.

And then the coat. If it isn't such to make him waterproof—insulated against all the elements—*it is not a Lab's coat!* And the way that coat *wraps* the tail is what allows the tail to become a distinguishing part of the silhouette.

The generic selection may have produced a well-made animal, but in ignoring the elements of type, what resulted could not possibly be considered a dog of great type.

(Linda Anderson photo)

(John Crook photo)

Type, type—who has the type?
Fallshort's Mister Blackie
Ch. Weathertop Storm Cloud

Pictured are two purebred Labrador Retrievers. Both trace back to blue-blooded ancestors. Which of the two has breed type? Hopefully, your choice will be Saudjie & John Crook's Ch. Weathertop Storm Cloud, the dog pictured on the bottom (facing page)! What does Storm Cloud have that his counterpart, Fallshort's Mister Blackie, lacks?

Breed character	Does Blackie look like the sturdy, strong-boned dog of substance that is, according to the standard, never long, tall, leggy in outline, or light and weedy?
Silhouette	Does Blackie's silhouette indicate he's that short-coupled, slightly longer-than-tall dog with great body capacity and good angles front and rear? Does his distinctive "otter" tail complete the outline you're looking for?
Head	If all you could see of Blackie was his head, would you know without question that he is a Labrador Retriever?
Movement	You can't know for sure how Blackie might move just by seeing his picture, but his poker-straight rear quarter and long legs might give you some indication.
Coat	The protective coat described in the standard and the manner in which that coat wraps the Labrador's tail are critical considerations in evaluating how the breed scores in this aspect of breed type. How does Blackie fare in these respects?

Now let's take a look at the picture of Ch. Storm Cloud. How does his picture score in respect to the five elements of breed type? I don't think you have to be a Labrador Retriever expert to determine that his final tally would be vastly superior to Blackie's. You could prop Storm Cloud's picture up beside the standard and follow along word for word. Does this make Storm Cloud the first perfect Lab? No. What it means is that he combines the five elements of breed type in such an excellent manner that there is no need to guess why we might say that he has breed type. Blackie is simply a generic version of the breed. He resembles the breed but lacks practically all the elements that stamp him as an example of quality. On the other hand, Storm Cloud does have the defining elements, but notice—not in excess! No "barrel on legs" here. His picture tells of an appropriately athletic dog whose physique equips him to participate in the most telling of canine decathlons.

Too much

Now looking at the opposite end of the evaluation spectrum, we see a trap the specialist might fall into. I shudder when I hear someone experienced and respected in the breed tell a novice that a Lab is simply head, coat, and tail—that little else matters.

The Lab's three defining characteristics are very important. There is no questioning that, but can anyone who loves and appreciates the Labrador Retriever discount everything else that makes this such a great breed? Head, coat, and tail, of course, but they are not *all* that a Lab is. The question must be asked—how far will head, coat, and tail take a dog that is of poor character, whose obese body is slung over dwarfed legs, and who is barely able to move out of its own way?

I exaggerate not! I've had breed specialists send that kind of dog to me in a Group! Good Labrador Retriever lovers, *that is not a typey specimen of the breed!* This flies in the face of the origin and purpose of the breed. This is not a dog that can do the job.

The Lab must be strong and of great body capacity, but at the same time he must be an athlete—suitable for the Decathlon. He must have endurance on land and water, combined with agility in both. What matter the perfect coat if elephantine weight carries him to the bottom of the lake or pond? What good are his lovely head and rudder tail if his legs are too short to pull him up the bank or carry his quarry over land?

The British often use the expression "stout fellow," and it may well apply to the Lab, but in the sense of robust and sturdy good health, rather than stout as in obese.

"The "Big Five" are the building blocks upon which the structure of the ideal Labrador Retriever is built. They are the same five upon which the Yorkie, the Great Dane, and the Bulldog are built. The Labrador Retriever is not some freak of nature— far from it. In his ideal form he stands as a model of canine perfection.

Developing a breed-type workbook

Hopefully what you've read in the preceding pages has shed some light on what it is you need to know in order to be able to appreciate a truly fine specimen in Labrador Retrievers or any other of our breeds. Now the task is collecting and recording all that information in such a manner that it can be referred to time and time again until it is committed to memory. Remember—the more information you accumulate under each of the five headings, the greater your appreciation of breed nuances, the more expert you become in making important decisions in a breed. The ideal dog in the whelping box or in the show ring is the dog that has most of what is itemized under each of the five elements of type.

If I were to ask you to sit down and write *everything* you know and would like to know about a breed, you might do that—when and if you had the time. But realistically, who in this day and age has that kind of time? It would probably remain on your "important things to do" list for a long, long time if not forever.

Having a place to jot down one important fact at a time about each element of breed type—and being able to find the information when you need it—would probably get my request out of "to do" and into *"done!"* Further, we don't learn everything at once—we learn a bit at a time.

What I advise my students to do is get an inexpensive standard-size looseleaf notebook and five divider tabs, allotting one tab for each of the five elements. Add some looseleaf paper for notes and some graph paper. I use the graph paper that has six squares to the inch because it allows me to record more detail.

This will become your "breed workbook." It will contain everything you find essential to a breed. This can be for your new breed or the one you've been involved in all your life. It's the place where the judge looks the night before judging that important entry and the same place the breeder refers to when evaluating that promising litter.

I can't tell you how many people who have attended my seminar come to me months later and say how much the process has helped them to put what is important in a breed into its proper perspective. They also tell me how many new things they have discovered or become more conscious of, even about breeds they've been involved in for many years.

Section 1—breed character

Let's start with the first element we looked at—breed character. As we've learned, breed character is the immediate impression a dog gives when it comes upon the scene. It's both physical and mental—static and kinetic. Do you want the light-footed style and grace of the Saluki, the power and majesty of the Great

Dane, or the muscular elegance and pride of self that marks the Doberman Pinscher?

This is also where you make notes on the amount of bone and substance that defines the breed. Over and over, the Papillon's standard stresses the breed's fine-boned structure and lightness of being. This is again both physical and mental. At the same time, the Pug, also a member of the Toy group, wants to be *"multum in parvo"*—much in little. This sturdy little fellow is twice his butterfly-like friend standing next to him in the Toy Group although in a package not all that much larger.

It's about attitude, demeanor, and carriage. It's what makes you think Cocker rather than Poodle. Breeders use the term "Poodley," "lordly" for the Chow Chow, and soulful for the Basset. What do these breed-specific terms mean to you?

Does the dog or puppy you are considering appeal by merit of its own breed character or through some generic qualities? How much can you concede to what is correct for the breed without giving away what makes *that breed distinctive*?

This is where you record this information.

Section 2—silhouette

When you looked at the picture of the Afghan Hound moving along the beach with its owner in Chapter 7, it is highly unlikely that you had any doubt in your mind as to what breed was portrayed. It isn't because the shot is up close and tight. You recognized the breed because of the dog's silhouette. That silhouette, like the correct silhouette for any purebred dog, defines its physicality by drawing a line around everything required by the standard. It reveals all the subtle and identifying curves and angles as the parts flow from one to the next.

This is where you begin to understand how important correct proportions are in creating a silhouette. Different standards have different ways of defining these proportions—some explicit, others somewhat vague. Some standards leave determining this vital information entirely up to the interested. Finding a method of charting what is correct that is applicable to all breeds can help us tremendously—not only in understanding the breed at hand but also in comparing different dogs in the breed to each other.

No breed has two or three correct silhouettes. Yes, some styles within a breed veer slightly to the right or the left of the ideal and are acceptable. However, this does not alter the fact that you must be totally conversant with the ideal.

Section 3—head

Once you are able to recognize the overall look and expression sought after in the breed being studied, this is the place where you will be noting the details that create this look: the ear make and shape that typifies; its relationship in respect to other prominent features of the head.

Sketching those relationships helps tremendously in that this simultaneously creates a fixed mental image that you will be using as a yardstick in making comparisons. First the whole, then the details within the whole, taking care to note the relationships of the details in the dogs whose heads are looked upon as outstanding.

Section 4—movement

On the first page of this section, print "THIS IS NOT A RACE" in large, bold capitals. This will help remind you that what you are attempting to learn is how this breed should move! This breed may be the slowest in its Variety Group. It may be the fastest. The important thing is that you keep your mind fixed on how history, tradition, the breed standard, and the construction of this breed should affect movement.

What about extension fore and aft? A little; a lot? What about lateral (rolling) motion—some, none? Single tracking?

All the notes and input you have on how the breed *should* move go here. Photos or sketches from magazine articles should be clipped and pasted in here. If you leave them in all the millions of monthlies that are published, you'll probably never get back to them, so clip and paste here!

Section 5—coat

Chapter 10 devoted considerable space to all the ramifications of coat. List all the characteristics that typify coat in the breed being studied. The coat requirements for some breeds touch upon all of this element's characteristics:

- Serviceability
- Texture
- Quality
- Pattern
- Color
- Trim
- Distribution
- Amount

How many apply directly to the coat of the breed you are working on?

Chapter 12 will assist you in defining these elements in a system I call "Graphing."

Here are exactly the same three Bichons that were pictured with their coats on in Chapter 10. Which did you choose as coming closest to the ideal silhouette? If you chose anything but Dog C, you were wrong. Many people who have been shown this example do choose the wrong dog. Why? One word—coat. In all fairness, pictures and drawings don't give you the opportunity to see beyond what the coat indicates is there. With living dogs before you, it then becomes your opportunity and your responsibility to determine if the dog is wearing the coat of if the coat is wearing the dog.

|12| The Graphing Technique

*T*his is where you will be using your graph paper. Take a sheet or two of the graph paper to your local copy center and have transparencies made. You'll use your paper for learning to visualize proportions and the transparencies to lay over pictures to see what proportions those past greats in your breed really had.

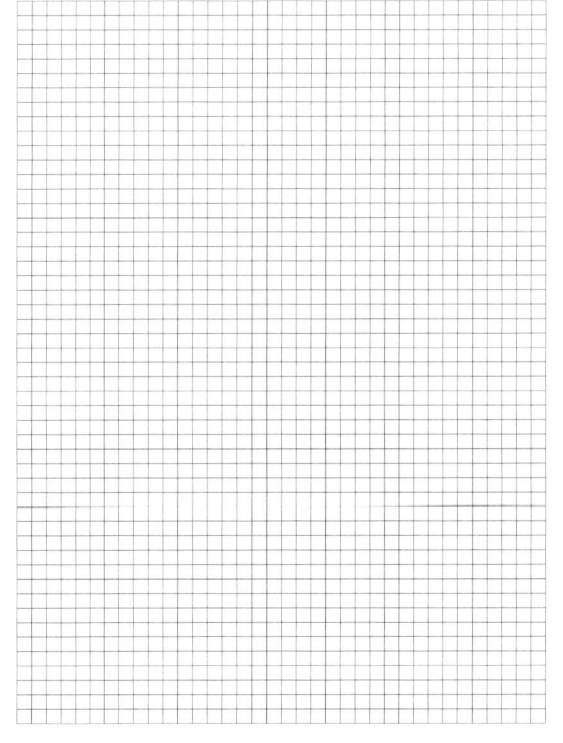

It's absolutely amazing what a great learning tool some inexpensive graph paper can be in helping you define type. You can use it to sketch on, and once you've had a transparency done of one of the graph sheets, it will reveal some very interesting things about the thousands of pictures that appear in the nation's dog press each month.

The silhouette used here was made from the photograph of the beautiful Bull Terrier bitch, Can. Am. Ch. Magor Maggie Mae, ROM. You will be drawing your own ideal silhouette from the proportions you find indicated in your standard and/or on the best dogs of your breed. You may well alter the picture somewhat here and there as time passes because you will begin to see that the best dogs may be a bit longer here, a bit shorter there.

This process has nothing to do with becoming an artist. Don't worry in the least about that. What you are doing is training yourself to recognize the ideal silhouette that proper proportions create and what is off when that ideal is not met. The more often you do this with quality dogs, the more finely honed your ability to *see* what's right becomes.

Let's take a look at Maggie Mae's silhouette. Lay your graph transparency over her picture and count the squares from breastbone to buttocks—*body length*. Compare that to the number of squares from withers to ground—*height*. What do you get from withers to set on of tail—(generally referred to as) *length of back*?

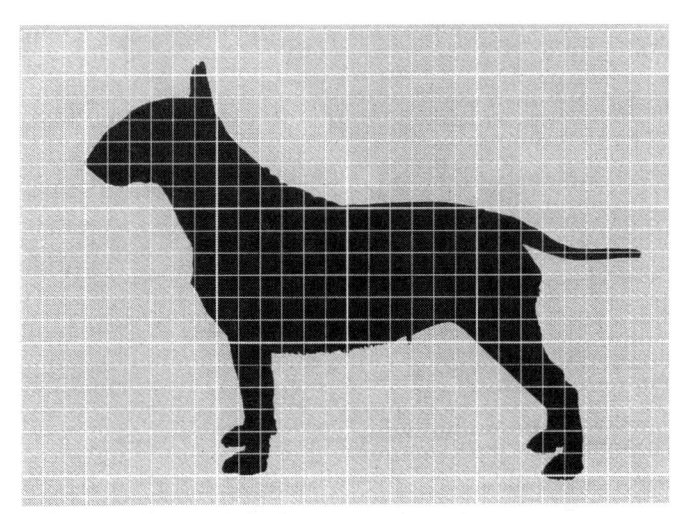

This is a silhouette drawn from the photograph of the Bull Terrier, Canadian and American Ch. Magor Maggie Mae, ROM, that appeared in Chapter 7. It's an ideal silhouette to work from in that there is nothing disguised by hair—what's there is there, pure and simple. You can use this silhouette to practice estimating proportions. The next step will be to sketch a silhouette (sans coat if yours is a coated breed) based on a dog or dogs in your breed that best represent the proportions called for in the standard. This exercise isn't intended to have you produce an artistic triumph—only to get your breed's proper proportions down on paper. If that appears beyond you, search out a silhouette from a book or magazine and copy that to work on. (Art courtesy of **Dogs In Canada***)*

You will also be able to calculate Maggie Mae's proportionate length of neck and depth of body (withers to bottom of chest). We will give greater detail to head further on, but it should be easy to see that you will also be able to graph length of head, distance from ear to eye—almost any portion of anatomy by using this method.

Understand that it is not the number of squares that is of consequence, or just what Maggie May's proportions are (unless you are a Bullie judge or breeder). The purpose of this exercise is train your eye to recognize how these measurements stand in proportion to each other. Time and repetition will not only help you develop recognition, they will commit to memory what outline you want the breed you are studying to have.

You will become accustomed to quickly noting if the dog you are looking at has enough length of body to accommodate its height at withers. Enough neck to be in correct balance. How much of the distance from withers to ground should be body and how much should be leg

After you have determined the correct overall silhouette, you can begin to put in the important details. For instance, how the breed's correct topline deviates, if it does, from dead level. Note Maggie Mae's topline is basically level, with only a gentle rise over the loin, returning to the low set on and downward journey of her tail. Her underline has its graceful upward curve.

Are the forequarters of your breed set forward as they are on the Smooth Fox Terrier pictured here, or does your breed stand over its front like this well-made German Shepherd Dog does?

Following a straight line drawn down from the rear-most point of Maggie Mae's buttocks, you will note that the line intersects the paw. Where does the rear foot of your breed set properly in relationship to that line? Where should it set? Is the line from hock to foot perpendicular to the ground, or does it slant forward (sickle hocked) or backward (weak and/or lacking angulation)? Where does the tail set on, and how is it carried?

Note how easy it becomes to determine proportions using this graphing procedure. Bit by bit, proportion by proportion, you will eventually have the ideal silhouette drawn in your notebook and eventually, and more importantly, imprinted in your mind.

As an example of how revealing the use of your graph transparency can be, we've superimposed a graph over the silhouettes of the two Clumber Spaniels that appear in Chapter 7. Starting at the same point on the forechest of each of the dogs, count the number of squares between there and the point of buttocks. Compare that to the number of squares you count from top of the shoulder to bottom of the foot. Can you now see why there is such a great difference in the silhouettes of these two dogs? Actually, the number of squares is irrelevant. This is simply an exercise that helps train your eye to detect the difference between right and wrong in a breed's silhouette. (Art courtesy of Dogs In Canada*)*

Is yours a coated breed? Hair is the first thing you want to eliminate. If you do not have an accurate picture of what the breed looks like without coat, you are never going to understand that breed. If you can't find cut-down dogs, you must have someone let you photograph the good ones when they are being bathed. Until you can see a dog through its coat, you aren't ready to breed or judge that breed.

Chapter 12   The Graphing Technique   215

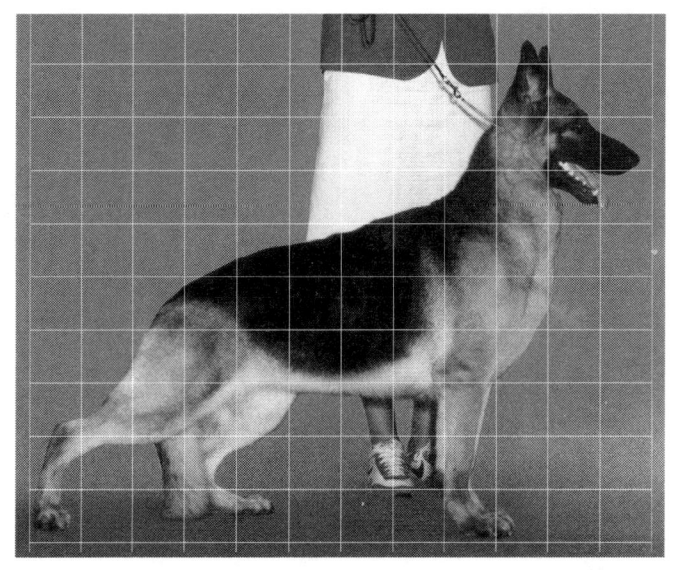

This technique can also assist a great deal in helping develop a sense of just where the parts within the framework of the silhouette belong. For instance, front construction in the breeds differs considerably, and these differences are a part of what constitutes type and affects proper movement within the individual breeds. Both the correct German Shepherd (above) and Smooth Fox Terrier (below) have well laid-back shoulders. The difference in their front construction lies in the length of their upper arms. The long upper arm of the German Shepherd allows her to stand well over her front—note how far the foreleg is set back from the forechest. The short upper arm of the Smooth Fox Terrier has the foreleg falling in what is almost a direct line down from the forechest. Both of these fronts are as they should be, and correctness of construction here provides each with the proper movement for its respective breed. Pictured: Bob and Carol Joseph's German Shepherd Ch. Lynrick's Crystle and Sergio Balcazar's Smooth Fox Terrier Ch. Son Es Alexander the Great. (Holloway photo)

Head

Exactly the same procedure you used to determine body proportions is used to better understand what is desired in respect to head. Using the graph we used for determining body proportions, we are quickly able to approximate muzzle to skull proportions in the profile of the Smooth Fox Terrier. Depth from top of skull to jaw junction can also be graphed—depth there relates to strength. What about these proportions in your breed?

Graphing helps immeasurably when looking at a dog head on. See how width of skull corresponds to length in the Wire Fox Terrier's head. Does the muzzle of the breed you are studying taper in width only slightly from under the eye to end of muzzle as it does here, or does it maintain that same width on down to the end of the muzzle as it does in the Chinese Shar-Pei?

Where in the skull should the eye be set in your breed—high or low? Where the eyes are placed is a good part of what produces the proper expression in a good many breeds and particularly the Dandie Dinmont, as we see in the classic head study of Ch. Montizard Kings Mtn Kricket.

How far apart should the eyes be placed? Are the eyes set dead level or obliquely? Where on the skull and in relationship to the eyes are the ears set? How close are the ears set, or are they set low on the sides of the skull? The ears of some breeds are set "well behind and just above" the level of the eye (Golden Retriever) or "no higher than a line to the lower part of the eye" (American Cocker Spaniel). Draw in where your breed's ear is set.

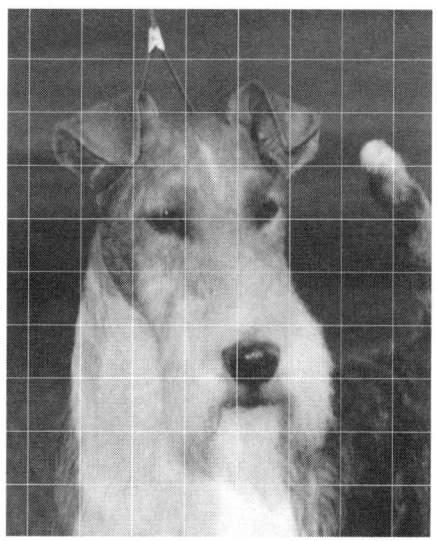

Regardless of breed, what you look for in defining type, surprisingly, remains very much the same. Where and how it appears is what creates type. Graphing will help you see whether or not what should be there actually is there. The Wire Fox Terrier (above) and Chinese Shar Pei (below) appear to have little or nothing in common until you start to look for what their standards ask for. Good length is important in both breeds. It's corresponding width that differs considerably. Ear set, size, and placement are critical in both breeds, and ear carriage represents a possible disqualification in both. Eye size, shape, and placement in the skull are essential considerations. Graphing can help you identify proportions and proportionate distances. Pictured are the Wire Fox Terrier Ch. Sunnybrook Spot On (Ludwig photo) and Chinese Shar Pei Down Homes Black Pearl. (Missy photo)

218   Solving the Mysteries of Breed Type

What can the use of the graphing technique tell you about these breeds?

Black and Tan Coonhound Ch. WyEast Wild Rose (Photo courtesy of Kathy Corbett)

Chesapeake Bay Retriever Ch. Ozark
Mt. Dare Devil (Heston photo)

Chapter 12 The Graphing Technique 219

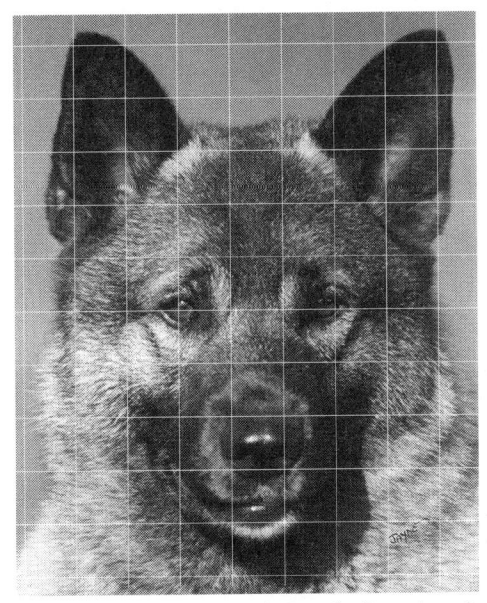

Norwegian Elkhound Ch. Vin Melca's Howdy Rowdy (Langdon photo)

Dandi Dinmont Terrier Ch. Montizard Kings Mtn. Kricket (Puig photo)

220   Solving the Mysteries of Breed Type

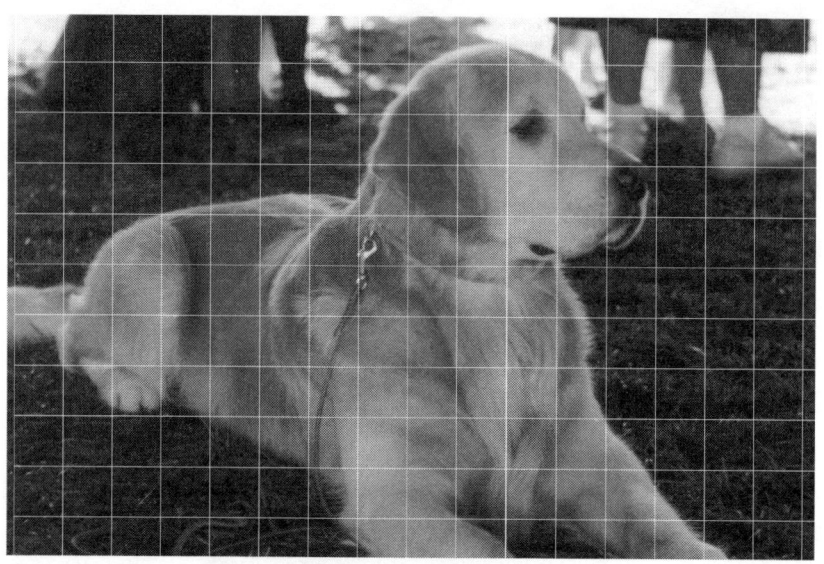

Golden Retriever Ch. Malagold Storm Warning

Cocker Spaniel Ch. Magicours Motorcade

Movement

Movement is a whole day and an entire lesson in itself for every breed, and that just gets us off the ground, so I'm not going to even try and cram what you'll need to know in that respect about your breed into a few pages. However, I cannot caution you enough in respect to those "three cardinal sins" in Chapter 9:

1. Confusing correct movement with showmanship.
2. Believing the basic principles governing canine locomotion produce only one kind of movement.
3. Not understanding that changing movement changes type.

Graphing can be of great assistance in developing an imprint of proper movement for your breed. Lay your graph over the spectacular movement photo of Pembroke Welsh Corgi, Can. Am. Ch. Fox Meadows Obsession. Note how easily she reaches beyond the vertical in front and rear. Also note how the rear pastern between hock and foot flexes and allows her to extend it rearward beyond the vertical.

The Corgi is a short-legged breed, but I can't help but marvel at the extent and ease of reach illustrated here. If she were a long-legged breed, that forward reach would extend well beyond her nose, an accomplishment that even the comparatively long-legged breeds required to move in this manner seldom achieve. The construction of the properly made Whippet couldn't depart much further from that of the proper Corgi's, but Ch. Sporting Field's Kinsman illustrates his breed has its own very measurable, very easy front and rear extension.

The common mistake made in evaluating movement is mistaking speed for reach (front) and drive (rear). American Cockers are fast indeed, and they can drive with all that angulation they have behind, but when you find a Cocker who can reach beyond his nose, you have witnessed something that has all but become a lost characteristic in the breed.

On the other hand, Bichons are inclined to fault at the rear end. The rear movement of far too many Bichons is entirely *under* the dog, and they are unable to flex that rear quarter out beyond the vertical, resulting in a stilted mincing movement.

222 Solving the Mysteries of Breed Type

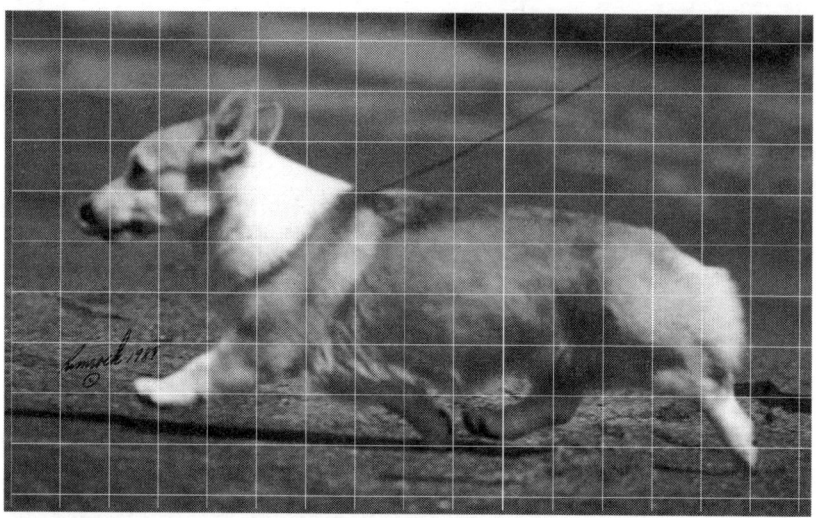

This classic Rimrock photo of Pembroke Welsh Corgi Ch. Fox Meadow's Obsession (above) illustrates everything the breed is capable of in respect to movement. Your overlay will give you the graphic illustration of what correct reach and drive for this short legged herding breed should be. Although constructed in a totally different manner than the Corgi, the Gilbert photo of Whippet Ch. Sporting Field's Kinsman (below) also provides us with very measurable front and rear extension.

Graphing where the legs should move forward and back from the vertical is what can help you recognize what is correct in your breed. Graphing can also help you determine how much convergence toward the center line you want when the dog comes and goes.

The broad chest of the Chow Chow permits little convergence of the forelegs as the dog moves toward you. On the other hand, the Shetland Sheepdog and Collie standard requires a distinct convergence both front and rear to the center line (single tracking) as speed increases.

After you have used the graphing technique over a period of time, you'll find yourself carrying it around with you mentally. You'll start superimposing it on living dogs and begin to see things that were previously obscure.

Looking through your imaginary graph as the Bulldog moves away, you begin to assess the breed's proper rolling movement by noting how much lateral displacement of the tail there is. The tail and therefore the whole rear end of the Bulldog "sashays" or rolls from right to left when the dog is moving properly.

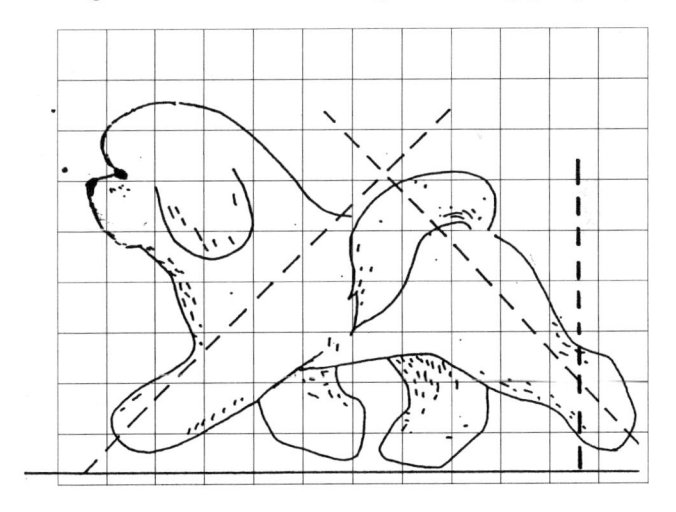

Recognizing rear quarter follow-through in the breeds that are required to have reach and drive can be somewhat difficult for some people. A graph overlay helps the eye recognize that the rear pastern, from hock to foot, must be able to flex beyond a vertical line in order to follow through and match the extension of the driving front quarter.

Using the graph over photographs of your own dog in motion can show you what others, including judges, see when the dog is moving. Is your breed required to move straight forward like the Chow Chow, Fox Terrier, or Bulldog? Or is there convergence to the center line like what is expected of the Shetland Sheepdog, German Shepherd, or German Shorthaired Pointer?

Coat

Coat is not something that can be graphed or, for that matter, effectively photographed. And, in truth, seeing is not necessarily believing. Most of what you will learn about coat is gained through touch. But that does not mean there is nothing to be included in your notes for this section.

Every standard imposes different emphasis on what you'll include under coat serviceability—texture, quality, pattern—as well as color, trim, and amount. Often texture varies with color, pattern evolves with age, and amount can mean too little or too much. Trimming can enhance or detract, and fads can create presentation that is entirely incorrect.

In summary

As you learn what is right and wrong—write it down! Even when the fault is worn by the best dog in the lineup and that is the dog you feel should win or the pup that should be retained, don't let those flaws go by without noting them.

Breed faults enter the picture subtly—just an occasional one here and there—but if judges and breeders don't pay attention, suddenly the breed is painted into a corner and there's no recourse: no dog to breed to that doesn't have that same problem lurking around in its pedigree.

Maintaining a "breed-type workbook" is a project that increases in value as the years go by and with the amount of material you enter. Remember, this is not an art project, only a reference work for yourself. Of course, you can share it with whomever you wish, but even then, getting the point across is of far greater consequence than rendering graphic perfection.

I only wish my mentors had recorded all their memories, dreams, and reflections. What great tools they would have been for all of us to use. Alas, in far too many cases, this was not so. Hopefully, the few of their gems of wisdom I have recorded here will provide the stepping stones for you, the reader, to carry on in their tradition of excellence.

Bibliography

Books

Allen, Michael. *The American Cocker Book*. Midway City, California: The American Cocker Magazine, 1989.

American Kennel Club. *The Complete Dog Book*. New York: Howell Book House, 1997.

Austin, Norman A. & Jean S. Austin. *The Complete American Cocker Spaniel*. New York: Howell Book House, 1993.

Beauchamp, Richard. *Breeding Dogs for Dummies*. New York: Hungry Minds, 2002.

Bichon Frise Club of America. *Illustrated Discussion of the Bichon Frise*. Centereach, New York: 32 Oak Street, 1988.

Bulldog Club of America Education Committee. *Illustrated Bulldog Conformation Guide*. Clayton, California: Bulldog Club of America, 1994.

Craig, Patricia. *Born to Win*. Phoenix, Arizona: Doral Publishing, Inc., 1997.

De Prisco, Andrew & James B. Johnson. *Choosing a Dog For Life*. Neptune City, New Jersey: T. F. H. Publications Inc., 1996.

Fiennes, Richard & Alice Fiennes. *The Natural History of Dogs*. Garden City, New York: The Natural History Press, 1970.

Fiorone, Fiorenzo. *The Encyclopedia of Dogs*. New York: Thomas Y. Crowell Company, 1970.

Gilbert, Edward M. Jr. & Thelma Brown. *K-9 Structure & Terminology*. New York: Howell Book House, 1995.

Grossman, Dr. Alvin. *The American Cocker Spaniel*. Phoenix, Arizona: Doral Publishing, Inc., 1988.

Hamilton, Ferelith & Arthur F. Jones, eds. *The World Encyclopedia of Dogs*. New English Library/Walter Parrish, 1971.

Hancock, Colonel David. *The Heritage of the Dog*. Alton, Hants, England: Nimrod Press Ltd., 1990.

Hastings, Pat & Erin Ann Rouse. *Tricks of the Trade*. Aloha, Oregon: Dogfolk Enterprises, 2000.

Milward, C. E. *Grenpark Fox Terriers*. Grenville Park, Pakenham, Australia: Cameron Milward, 1990.

Oppenheimer, R. H. *After Bar Sinister*. Ashford, Kent, England: Dog World, 1969.

Oppenheimer, R. H. *McGuffin and Company*. Ashford, Kent, England: Dog World,1964.

Sefton, Frances. *The Lhasa Apso*. Spit Junction, New South Wales, Australia: Swales & Co., 1970.

Serpell, James. *The Domestic Dog*. Cambridge, England: Cambridge University Press,1995.

Smythe, R. H. *The Breeding and Rearing of Dogs*. New York: Arco Publishing Co. Inc.,1969.

Spira, Harold R., D.V.M. *Canine Terminology*. Sydney, Australia: Harper & Row Publishers,1982.

Stockmann, Friederun. (Translated from the German by E. Fitch Daglish) *My Life With Boxers*. New York: Coward-McCann Inc., 1961.

Wagner, John P. *The Boxer*. New York: Orange Judd Publishing Co. Inc., 1939.

Williams, Mary Roslin. *Advanced Labrador Breeding*. London: H. F. & G. Witherby Ltd.1988 (Also published as *Reach for the Stars*. Phoenix, Arizona: Doral Publishing Inc.,) 2000.

Magazines

AKC Gazette
260 Madison Avenue
New York, NY 10016
(800) 533-7323

Dog World
9 Tufton Street
Ashford, Kent TN23 6LW
England

Kennel Review Magazine
1241 Knollwood Drive, PMB 4
Cambria, CA 93428

Bloodlines
United Kennel Club
100 E. Kilgore Road
Kalamazoo, MI 49002

Dogs In Canada
Canadian Kennel Club
89 Skyway Avenue #200
Etobicoke, Ontario
Canada M9W 6R4

Purebred Dogs in Review
P.O. Box 30430
Santa Barbara, CA 93130

Videos

AKC and the Sport of Dogs, American Kennel Club
Dog Steps, Rachel Page Elliot, American Kennel Club
Puppy Puzzle, Pat Hastings, Dogfolk Enterprises
Breed Standard Videos, American Kennel Club

Web Sites

American Kennel Club
    www.akc.org
American Rare Breed Association
    www.arba.org
Australian National Kennel Council
    www.ankc.aust.com.
Canadian Kennel Club
    www.ckc.ca/info
The Kennel Club (England)
    www.the-kennel-club.org.uk
United Kennel Club
    www.ukcdogs.com
Federation Cynologique Internationale
    www.fci.be/english

Index

A
Ch. Acadia Command Performance 85
Accuracy 7
    education 9
    efficient use of time 13
    interpretation 9
    preference 7
Advertising, its effects 22
Ch. Altana's Mystique 66, 175
Anderson, Rosalie 36
Azaline White Witch of Piketberg 160

B
Ch. Banchory Orange Chiffon 162
Ch. Banchory Thousands Cheered 76
Ch. Bandog's Crawdaddy Gumbo 98
Ch. Beau Monde Miss Chaminade 114
Ch. Beau Monde More Paint 36
Ch. Beau Monde War Paint 152
Beauty points 77
Ch. Bel S'mbran Bachrach 97
Ch. Bel S'mbran Promise of Attalah 46
Ch. Bel S'mbran Fantasia xvii
Ch. Bellacairn's Bit O'Scotch 163
Bengston, Bo iv
Ch. Berlane's Causin' An Uproar 127
Bichon Frise Club of America 111
Billings, Michelle 60
Ch. Black Panther of Cad 175
Ch. Blackpool Crinkle Forest 117
Blossom 167
Books 5
Ch. Braegate Model of Bellhaven xii
Breed character 85, 88 - 89, 93, 207
Breed development 113, 120
Breed progress triad 23, 30
Breed standards 4, 23, 68
Breed type 205

    assessing 82
    breed character 85
    characteristics 84
    coat 87
    elements of 85, 88
    essentials 3
    head 86, 142
    movement 87
    research 4
    silhouette 86
    workbook 202, 206
Briggs, Simon xvi
Ch. Brunswig's Cryptonite 34

C
Ch. Chaminade Mr. Beau Monde 139, 196
Ch. Chik T' Sun of Caversham xv
Ch. Clussexx Billy Goat's Gruff 61, 154
Ch. Clussexx Three D Grinchey Glee 66
Ch. Courtenay Fleetfoot of Pennyworth 61, 70
Ch. Coy's Top Of The Mark 47
Character 20
Clark, Anne Rogers 33
Clumber Spaniel 123
Coad, Michael xvi
Coat 87 - 88, 183, 209
    amount 191
    color 188
    graphing 225
    markings 188, 196
    pattern and distribution 187
    texture 25
    trim 189
Corish, Geoff xvi

D

Ch. Dau Han's Dan Morgan 63
Dandie Dinmont 126
Davey, Betty 128
Ch. Devon's Puff and Stuff 89
Ch. Dhandy's Favorite Woodchuck 101
Dondino, Paolo xviii
Down Homes Black Pearl 145, 217
Draper, Dr. Samuel 47
Ch. Dreamridge Dear Charles 152
Ch. Dreamridge Dear Daphne 173
Ch. Drewlaine Eau de Love 154
Ch. Dunelm Galaxy 59
Ch. Dynamic Super Sensation 151
Ch. Dynasty's Speaking Of Him 49

E

Education and accuracy 9
Ch. El-bo's Rudy Is A Dandy 65
Elements of breed type 88
Ch. Evergreen Best Kept Secret 162
Ch. Evergreen Chase The Clouds 141, 162
Expression 147

F

Fallshort's Mister Blackie 205
Federacion Cynologique Internationale xxi
Ch. Feinlyne Femme Fatale 192
Ch. Fox Meadows Obsession 221
Ch. Fraja EC Winning Ticket 119

G

Ch. Glenhaven Lord Jack 149
Ch. Guardstock Red Atom 119
Godsol, Beatrice iii, 16, 83
Ch. Golden Hills I Love You Ashley 106
Graphing
    movement 221
    silhouette 212
    the coat 225
    the head 216
Graphing technique 211
Groskin, Gladys R. 64

H

Head 86, 146, 209, 216
    and expression 88, 147
    ear placement 161
    emphasis 155
    shape 157
    types 150
Ch. Hilltop's S. S. Cheese Cake 105
Ch. Hollyfir's Poacher's Pocket of Piketberg 117
Honesty
    and advertising 22
    character 20
    courage of convictions 19
    prejudicial conduct 21
    roadblocks 21
Hoyt, Hayes Blake 55

I

Ch. Innisfree Sierra Cinnar 25
Ch. Iowana's Fancy Flair 119

J

Jarvinen, Kari xviii

K

Ch. Kabik's the Challenger 62, 86
Ch. Kennoway Bill Bailey 79
Khan, Keke 46
Kinvale Can Do 162
Ch. Kishniga Desert Song 104, 171
Ch. Kishniga Dalgarth 104
Krause, Dr. Alvin 76

L

Lehtinen, Hans xviii, 174
Lennard, Susan B. 51
Lipiane, Paul iv
Livestock judges 6
Logical conclusions 15
Long and low 131
Ch. Longleat Alimor Raisin' Cane 102
Eng. Ch. Longcrag Archimedes 101
Lummelampi, Chris 174
Ch. Lynrick's Crystle 215

M

Mackay-Smith, Mrs. W. E. 159
Ch. Magicours Motorcade 220

Ch. Magor Maggie Mae 126, 212
Ch. Malagold Storm Warning 220
Markings 188, 196
Mason, Charles 17
Ch. McCammon's Marquis 60, 70
Mentors 83-84
Messinger, Frances 39
Mij Charbonneau's "Budkis" 161
Ch. Montizard King's Mtn. Kricket 86
Ch. Montizard Kings Mtn. Kricket 219
Movement 48, 87 - 88, 165, 174, 209
    cardinal sins of 168
    graphing 221
Ch. Mr. Stewart's Cheshire Winslow 60, 70
Ch. Mysti's Triumph of Valley Run 170

N
Ch. Nautilus Saltwater Sugar Buoy 102
Ch. Nebriowa Paper Maché 111
Int. Ch. Nunsoe Duc de la Terrace of Blakeen 55

O
Objectivity 17
Ch. Ophaal Of Crown Crest 109
Ch. Ozark Mt. Dare Devil 218
Ch. Ozark Mt. Daredevil 78

P
Piketberg Sensation 160
Points of beauty 78
Popular Mechanics approach 35
Preference 7
Prejudicial conduct 21

Q
Ch. Quailmoor Jumpin' Jack Flash 8
Quintus v. Bergherbus 194

R
Ch. Ralanda Ami Pierre 164
Rand, Vicki iv
Rayne, Derek iii, 62, 83
Relationship of breeder and judge 29
Reznik, Allan iv
Riddle, Maxwell 98
Ch. Rimskittle Ruffian 201

Ringside observations 10, 39
Roberts, Percy 30
Ch. Rock Falls Colonel xiv, 35
Ch. Rock Ledge Mac Michael 59, 69
Rosenberg, Alva 62
Ch. RRR's Super Samson 53

S
Ch. Sakkhara's Pharaoh 183
Ch. Salilyn's Aristocrat 62, 70
Ch. Sand Island Small Kraft Lite 76
Ch. Sequani's Dana Macduff 124
Serviceability 184
Shape of head 157
Ch. Sheen Von Westphalen 125
Ch. Sheenwater Gamble On Me 99
Silhouette 86, 88, 110, 120, 124, 128, 130, 208
    and anatomy 133
    common expressions 133
    disguises 138
    graphing 212
Skarda, Langdon 59
Ch. Smoke N' Mirrors 162
Sound evaluation essentials 6
Sound reasons 23
    in assisting breeders 26
    in assisting judges 24
Ch. Son Es Alexander the Great 215
Ch. Sunnybrook Spot On 217
Spira, Harry xvi
Ch. Sporting Field's Kinsman 221
Standards, breed 4
Starbeck Silken Starshine 151
Statistics 67, 69
Ch. St. Aubrey's Dragonora Of Elsdon 64
Stephenson, Mary N. 53
Stevenson, Ann xvi
Sunnybank Collies x
Sutton, "Beefy" xvi
Sutton, Catherine xvi - xvii
Systematic elimination 10

T
Ch. Tal-E-Ho's Top Banana 39
Tamarin Red Velvet Foon Ying 194
Tamkin Brave Beauty 153
Tauskey, Rudolf 142 - 143

Terhune, Albert Payson x
Ch. Timothy's Sparkle Plenty 149
Ch. Tonatron Glory Lass 100
Touch-ups 142
Trotter, Patricia Craige 63
Ch. Troymere Believe In Me 139
Ch. Tsar Shadow's The Berserker 107
Ch. Ttarb the Brat 11, 65
Ch. TuRo's Futurian Of Cachet 64
Type
    definition 51 - 52, 56
    interpretation 55 - 56
    opinion 56
    within breed 49
Type factor 45
Type vs. Soundness 44 - 45, 47

U
Use of time 13

V
Ch. Vin Melca's Howdy Rowdy 219
Ch. Vin Melca's Vagabond 63
Voorhinen, Reiner xviii, 65

W
Ch. Wah-Hu Redcloud Sugar Daddy 194
Ch. Weathertop Storm Cloud 205
Ch. Weeblu's Trailblazer of Don-El 193
Wentzle Ruml III 104
Ch. Westfield's Cunomorous Stone 58
Williams, Mary Roslin 16
Ch. Windarla's World Seeker 195
Ch. Winterfold Bold Bid 125
Ch. WyEast Wild Rose 218

Y
Ch. Yojimbo's Orion 167